Oxford AQA GCSE History (9-1)

Britain: Power and People c1170-Present Day

Revision Guide

 RECAP  APPLY  REVIEW ✓ SUCCEED

 UPDATED

Changes to the AQA GCSE History specification 8145 (Version 1.3) and support for these changes

AQA released Version 1.3 of their AQA GCSE History specification in September 2019. The changes are to the command words and stems to a number of the AQA GCSE History questions to make the demands of the questions clearer for all students. Please refer to the AQA website for more information.

To support you with these changes, we have reviewed the content of this book and made the necessary small amends.

SERIES EDITOR
Lindsay Bruce   Aaron Wilkes

OXFORD

Great Clarendon Street, Oxford, OX2 6DP, United Kingdom

Oxford University Press is a department of the University of Oxford.

It furthers the University's objective of excellence in research, scholarship, and education by publishing worldwide. Oxford is a registered trade mark of Oxford University Press in the UK and in certain other countries.

© Oxford University Press 2018

The moral rights of the authors have been asserted.

First published in 2018

Revised impression 2020

British Library Cataloguing in Publication Data

Data available

978-0-19-843290-6

Digital edition 978-0-19-843291-3

9 10 8

Paper used in the production of this book is a natural, recyclable product made from wood grown in sustainable forests.

The manufacturing process conforms to the environmental regulations of the country of origin.

Printed in China by Shanghai Offset Printing Products Ltd

Acknowledgements

Cover: Portrait of Oliver Cromwell (1599–1658) 1649 (oil on canvas), Walker, Robert (1607–60)/Leeds Museums and Galleries (Leeds Art Gallery) U.K./Bridgeman Images

Artworks: QBS Learning

Photos: p13: British Library; **p27:** The Pope suppressed by King Henry VIII, 1534 (engraving) (b/w photo), English School, (16th century)/Private Collection/Bridgeman Images; **p29:** Timewatch Images Stock Photo/Alamy Stock Photo; **p39:** John Leech/ Cartoon Stock; **p41:** Universal History Archive/Getty Images; **p47:** London Dock Strike, 1889 (b/w photo), English Photographer, (19th century)/Private Collection/ Bridgeman Images; **p49:** Everett Collection Inc Stock Photo/Alamy Stock Photo; **p55:** British Cartoon Archive/Solo Syndication; **p58:** Everett Collection/Mary Evans

The publisher would like to thank Jon Cloake for his work on the Student Book on which this Revision Guide is based, and Ellen Longley for reviewing this Revision Guide.

We are grateful to the Trustees of the Estate of Enoch Powell for permission to include an extract from Enoch Powell's speech delivered to the Conservative Association Meeting in Birmingham, 20 April 1968.

We have made every effort to trace and contact all copyright holders before publication. If notified of any errors or omissions, the publisher will be happy to rectify these at the earliest opportunity.

Links to third party websites are provided by Oxford in good faith and for information only. Oxford disclaims any responsibility for the materials contained in any third party website referenced in this work.

From the author, Lindsay Bruce: I would like to thank Liz Hammond and Melanie Waldron for their support and guidance; without them this Revision Guide would make very little sense! My thanks must also go to Aaron Wilkes, Janice Chan, Jon Cloake and the team at OUP. Lastly, thank you to my husband, who did way more bedtimes than me while I wrote this – I love you.

Contents

Part one:

Challenging authority and feudalism

			RECAP	APPLY	REVIEW

Part two:

Challenging royal authority

Contents

Introduction

The *Oxford AQA GCSE History* textbook series has been developed by an expert team led by Jon Cloake and Aaron Wilkes. This matching revision guide offers you step-by-step strategies to master your AQA Thematic Study: Power and the People exam skills, and the structured revision approach of **Recap, Apply and Review** to prepare you for exam success.

Use the **Progress checklists** on pages 3–4 to keep track of your revision, and use the traffic light feature on each page to monitor your confidence level on each topic. Other exam practice and revision features include **Top revision tips** on page 6, and the **'How to...'** guides for each exam question type on pages 7–9.

RECAP Each chapter recaps key events and developments through easy-to-digest chunks and visual diagrams. **Key terms** appear in bold and red; they are defined in the glossary. indicates the relevant Oxford AQA History Student Book pages so you can easily re-read the textbook for further revision.

SUMMARY highlights the most important facts at the end of each chapter.

TIMELINE provides a short list of dates to help you remember key events.

APPLY Each revision activity is designed to help drill your understanding of facts, and then progress towards applying your knowledge to exam questions.

These targeted revision activities are written specifically for this guide, which will help you apply your knowledge towards the four exam questions in your AQA Power and the People exam paper:

SOURCE ANALYSIS   **EXPLAIN THE SIGNIFICANCE**   **SIMILARITY/DIFFERENCE**   **FACTORS**

 Examiner Tip highlights key parts of an exam question, and gives you hints on how to avoid common mistakes in exams.

 Revision Skills provides different revision techniques. Research shows that using a variety of revision styles can help cement your revision.

 Review gives you helpful reminders about how to check your answers and how to revise further.

REVIEW Throughout each chapter, you can review and reflect on the work you have done, and find advice on how to further refresh your knowledge.

You can tick off the Review column from the Progress checklist as you work through this revision guide. **Activity answers guidance** and the **Exam practice** sections with full sample student answers also help you to review your own work.

Top revision tips

Getting your revision right

It is perfectly natural to feel anxious when exam time approaches. The best way to keep on top of the stress is to be organised!

3 months to go

Plan: create a realistic revision timetable, and stick to it!

Track your progress: use the Progress checklists (pages 3–4) to help you track your revision. It will help you stick to your revision plan.

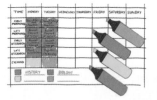

Be realistic: revise in regular, small chunks, of around 30 minutes. Reward yourself with 10 minute breaks – you will be amazed how much more you'll remember.

Positive thinking: motivate yourself by turning your negative thoughts to positive ones. Instead of asking *'why can't I remember this topic at all?'* ask yourself *'what different techniques can I try to improve my memory?'*

Organise: make sure you have everything you need – your revision books, coloured pens, index cards, sticky notes, paper, etc. Find a quiet place where you are comfortable. Divide your notes into sections that are easy to use.

Timeline: create a timeline with colour-coded sticky notes, to make sure you remember important dates relating to the four parts of the Power and the People Thematic Study (use the Timeline on page 11 as a starting point).

Practise: ask your teachers for practice questions or past papers.

Revision techniques

Using a variety of revision techniques can help you remember information, so try out different methods:

- Make **flashcards**, using both sides of the card to test yourself on key figures, dates, and definitions
- **Colour-code** your notebooks
- **Reread** your textbook or copy out your notes
- Create **mind-maps** for complicated topics
- Draw **pictures** and symbols that spring to mind
- Group study
- Find a **buddy** or group to revise with and test you
- Listen to revision **podcasts** or watch revision **clips**
- Work through the **revision activities** in this guide.

Revision tips to help you pass your Power and the People exam

1 month to go

Key concepts: make sure you understand key concepts for this topic, such as royal authority, protest, rebellion and democracy. If you're unsure, attend revision sessions and ask your teacher.

Identify your weaknesses: which topics or question types are easier and which are more challenging for you? Schedule more time to revise the challenging topics or question types.

Make it stick: find memorable ways to remember chronology, using fun rhymes, or doodles, for example.

Take a break: do something completely different during breaks – listen to music, take a short walk, make a cup of tea, for example.

Check your answers: answer the exam questions in this guide, *then* check the Activity answers guidance at the end of the guide to practise applying your knowledge to exam questions.

Understand your mark scheme: review the Mark schemes (page 10) for each exam question, and make sure you understand how you will be marked.

Master your exam skills: study and remember the How to master your exam skills steps (pages 7–9) for each AQA question type – it will help you plan your answers quickly!

Time yourself: practise making plans and answering exam questions within the recommended time limits.

Take mock exams seriously: you can learn from them how to manage your time better under exam conditions.

Rest well: make sure your phone and laptop are put away at least an hour before bed. This will help you rest better.

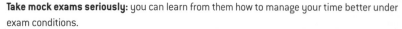

On the big day

Sleep early: don't work through the night; get a good night's sleep.

Be prepared: make sure you know where and when the exam is, and leave plenty of time to get there.

Check: make sure you have all your equipment in advance, including spare pens!

Drink and eat healthily: avoid too much caffeine or junk food. Water is best – if you are 5% dehydrated, then your concentration drops 20%.

Stay focused: don't listen to people who might try to wind you up about what might come up in the exam – they don't know any more than you.

Good luck!

Master your exam skills

Get to grips with your Paper 2: Power and the People Thematic Study

The Paper 2 exam lasts 2 hours, and you have to answer eight questions covering two topics. The first four questions (worth 40 marks) will cover the Thematic Study; the last four questions (40 marks) will cover your British Depth Study topic. Here, you will find details about what to expect from the first four questions which relate to the Thematic Study topic Power and the People, and advice on how to master your exam skills.

You should spend about 50 minutes in total on the Power and the People questions – see pages 8–9 for how long to spend on each question.

The four questions will always follow this pattern:

▼ **SOURCE A**

1 Study **Source A**. How useful is **Source A** to a historian studying ...? Explain your answer using **Source A** and your contextual knowledge.   8 marks

2 Explain the significance of ...   8 marks

3 Explain two ways in which ... and ... were similar/different.   8 marks

4 Has ... been the main factor in ...? Explain your answer with reference to ... and other factors.   16 marks   SPaG 4 marks

REVISION SKILLS

Read the *British Depth Study Revision Guide* for help on the last four questions of Paper 2.

EXAMINER TIP

Remember that this question is similar to the source question in Paper 1, but this focuses on just *one* source.

EXAMINER TIP

This question requires you to think about the significance of something. You have to consider the contemporary, short- and long-term impact of an event or development.

EXAMINER TIP

This question is worth a lot of marks and requires a longer answer. Make sure you leave plenty of time to complete it at the end of the exam. Don't forget that you get up to 4 marks for spelling, punctuation and grammar (SPaG) on this question too.

REVIEW

If you find FACTORS challenging, look out for the **FACTORS** activities throughout this guide to help you revise and drill your understanding of the FACTORS questions. Look out for the **REVISION SKILLS** tips too, to inspire you to find the revision strategies that work for you!

How to master the 'source' question

This question targets your understanding of how useful this source is to a historian. Usually, the source will be an image (a cartoon or drawing, for example), but in some years a textual source may be used. Here are the steps to consider when answering the source question.

Question 1

- **Content:** Look at the source carefully. What point is the artist or writer making about the subject? Circle or underline any key points or arguments that are made.

- **Provenance:** Consider the time in which the source was created. What topic or event does the source relate to? Use the provenance (caption) of the source to think about where the source was created, the circumstances of the creator, how much information they had, and their purpose and audience.

- **Context:** Now think back over your own knowledge. Write about whether the content and caption fit with what you know. Does it give a fair reflection of the person, event or issue it describes?

- **Comment:** You need to make a judgement about how useful the source is. A good way to work towards an answer is to think about what is 'inside' the source (that may be the image or text) and what is 'outside' the source (the provenance). These two pieces of information affect the usefulness of a source for a historian studying a particular topic.
- ⏱ Spend about 10 minutes answering this 8-mark question.

How to master the 'significance' question

Judging the significance of a person or event is about looking at the impact that the person/event had *at the time*, how it affected people *in the long term*, and whether it is still relevant *today*. Here are the steps to consider for answering the 'significance' question.

Question 2

- **Plan:** Consider the immediate importance or impact (short term) of a person/event and their importance later on (long term). Look at the diagram carefully to help you plan:

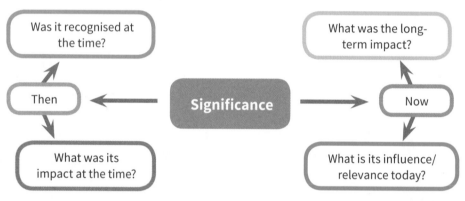

- **Explain the significance:** You need to say what *impact* the event/feature/person made, and whether it had an impact at the time and/or now. In what ways did it have an impact on the wider historical period? Did it affect people's lives? Did it have an impact on politics or the government? Did it lead to change? What happened as a result of it?
- ⏱ Spend about 10 minutes answering this 8-mark question.

How to master the 'similarity/difference' question

Here are the steps to consider for answering the 'similarity/difference' question. This question asks you to consider the similarities or differences between two events or developments.

Question 3

- **Plan**: Make a list or a mind-map to help you analyse the similarities or differences between the two events/developments. What historical facts do you know about the similarities or differences for each of the events/developments?
- **Write**: When you have chosen two similarities or differences you want to write about, organise them into two paragraphs, one for each. Consider these points for each paragraph:
  - **Causes:** think about the ways in which the two events have similar or different causes.

- • **Development:** consider what you know about what happened in both events. Look for points of similarity or difference that you can identify and explain.
  - • **Consequences:** think about the results of the events – again identify and explain similarities or differences.
- • ⏱ Spend about 10 minutes answering this 8-mark question.

How to master the 'main factors' question

The last question on Power and the People in Paper 2 is a question on 'main factors'. It carries the highest mark, along with 4 marks for spelling, punctuation and grammar. The question gives you the opportunity to 'show off' your knowledge of the whole Power and the People Thematic Study and select information that shows the influence of factors in history, such as religion, war, chance, government, communication, science and technology, and the role of the individual.

Question 4

- • **Read the question carefully:** The question will name one factor. Circle the named factor. What topic is the question asking you to consider? The topic is located at the end of the first sentence. Underline the topic to help you focus your answer.
- • **Plan your essay:** You could plan your essay by listing the named factor and other factors that caused the event/issue stated in the question:

Named factor 1	Another factor 2	Another factor 3

Write in anything you could use as evidence for the different factors, but make sure that your answer is relevant to the topic of the Thematic Study that has been asked in the question (the one you underlined).

- • **Write your essay:** Aim for about four paragraphs. First, write about the influence of the named factor in relation to the topic asked in the question. Write a paragraph each about two more factors in addition to the one named in the question. Lastly, you will have to come to a judgement (a clear conclusion) about whether you agree that the named factor was the main factor. Try to weigh up the named factor against the other ones you wrote about, and say which was more important.
- • **Check your SPaG:** Don't forget that you get up to 4 marks for your SPaG in this answer. It's a good idea to leave time to check your SPaG.
- • ⏱ This question is worth 16 marks plus 4 SPaG marks. Spend around 20 minutes on it, but this needs to include time to plan and to check your SPaG.

EXAMINER TIP

Remember that you only have about 2–3 minutes to plan and 15–17 minutes to write your paragraphs. For each factor, choose two historical facts from the history of Power and the People you are most confident about, and highlight these.

EXAMINER TIP

To back up your conclusion, you should explain *why* you came to that judgement, with supporting evidence. Answers that demonstrate a broad knowledge of examples from across the whole Thematic Study are more likely to gain higher marks.

EXAMINER TIP

Don't forget you will have to answer 4 more questions, relating to your British Depth Study topic, in Paper 2. Ensure you leave enough time to complete both sections of Paper 2! You are advised to spend 50 minutes on your British Depth Study.

REVIEW

You can find sample student answers to each question type in the Exam practice pages at the end of this Revision Guide.

AQA GCSE History mark schemes

Below are simplified versions of the AQA mark schemes, to help you understand the marking criteria for your **Paper 2 Britain: Power and the People Thematic Study** exam.

Level	Question 1 Source question
4	• Complex evaluation of the source • Argument is shown throughout the answer about how useful the source is, supported by evidence from provenance *and* content, and relevant facts 7–8 marks
3	• Developed evaluation of the source • Argument is stated about how useful the source is, supported by evidence from source content and/or provenance 5–6 marks
2	• Simple evaluation of the source • Answer is shown about how useful the source is, based on content and/or provenance 3–4 marks
1	• Basic analysis of the source • Basic description of the source is shown 1–2 marks

Level	Question 2 Significance question
4	• Complex explanation of aspects of significance • A range of accurate, detailed and relevant facts are shown 7–8 marks
3	• Developed explanation of aspects of significance • A range of accurate, relevant facts are shown 5–6 marks
2	• Simple explanation of one aspect of significance • Specific relevant facts are shown 3–4 marks
1	• Basic explanation of aspect(s) of significance • Some basic related facts are shown 1–2 marks

Level	Question 3 Similarity/difference question
4	• Complex explanation of similarities or differences • A range of accurate, detailed and relevant facts are shown 7–8 marks
3	• Developed explanation of similarities or differences • A range of accurate, relevant facts are shown 5–6 marks
2	• Simple explanation of one similarity or difference • Specific relevant facts are shown 3–4 marks
1	• Basic explanation of similarity or difference • Some basic related facts are shown 1–2 marks

Level	Question 4 Main factors question
4	• Complex explanation of named factor *and* other factor(s) • Argument is shown throughout the structured answer, supported by a range of accurate, detailed and relevant facts 13–16 marks
3	• Developed explanation of the named factor *and* other factor(s) • Argument is shown throughout the structured answer, supported by a range of accurate and relevant facts 9–12 marks
2	• Simple explanation of the stated factor or other factor(s) • Argument is shown, supported by relevant facts 5–8 marks
1	• Basic explanation of one or more factors • Some basic facts are shown 1–4 marks

You also achieve up to 4 marks for spelling, punctuation and grammar (SPaG) on the main factors question:

Level	Question 4 Main factors question SPaG marks
Excellent	• SPaG is accurate throughout the answer • Meaning is very clear • A *wide* range of key historical terms are used accurately 4 marks
Good	• SPaG shown with considerable accuracy • Meaning is generally clear • A range of key historical terms are used 2–3 marks
Satisfactory	• SPaG shown with some accuracy • SPaG allows historical understanding to be shown • Basic historical terms are used 1 mark

Britain: Power and the People c1170–Present Day Timeline

The colours represent different types of event as follows:

Blue: political   Black: war/rebellion

Purple: religious   Green: social

1215		Magna Carta is signed by King John
1265		Simon de Montfort calls a parliament that has 'commoners' in it
1295		Edward I calls the Model Parliament, which resembles ours today
1381		Local uprisings lead to the Peasants' Revolt; the leader, Wat Tyler, is killed
1536–37		People from the north of England start a pilgrimage to protest about King Henry VIII's changes to the Church
1642–51		English Civil War occurs between those who support King Charles I and those who support parliament
1649		Charles I is executed and Oliver Cromwell takes power
1649–60		Cromwell leads the Commonwealth
1775–82		Britain's defeat in War of Independence results in the loss of the American colonies
1804		Slave rebellion in St Dominique leads to the creation of the new independent state of Haiti
1819		Peterloo Massacre: protestors demanding the vote are attacked by the authorities
1832		Great Reform Act is passed
1833		Factory Reform Act reduces the amount of hours women and children can work
1834		Tolpuddle Martyrs are arrested for holding a union meeting
1846		Corn Laws are repealed
1838–48		Chartism movement tries to secure more representation for the working class
1897		National Union of Women's Suffrage Societies is set up; the campaign for women's suffrage becomes organised
1918		Women over 30 get the vote
1926		General Strike takes place in support of British miners
1928		Women get the vote on the same terms as men; there is universal suffrage
1948		*Empire Windrush* arrives in Britain, beginning a new wave of West Indian migration to the country
1981		Brixton Riots take place and lead to the Scarman Report into institutional racism in the police

 **RECAP**

Medieval society

Medieval society was built on the **feudal system**.

- The king was at the top of this system.
- The king gave land to the **barons**.
- The barons gave the king money and men to fight in wars.
- Knights were given land if they promised to fight when needed.

Under the feudal system the king had the final say. Kings were supposed to listen to the Great Council (a group of trusted advisors) – but they rarely did.

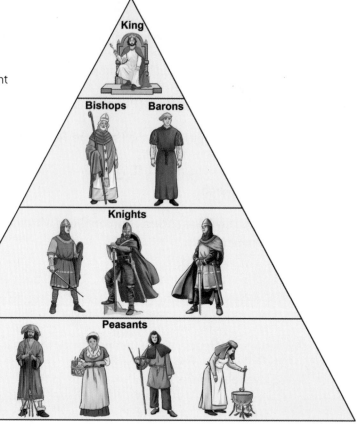

King John

A Medieval king was meant to:

- defend the people by leading the army well
- keep the country peaceful
- successfully deal with any rebellions
- maintain good relations with the Church and the Pope.

Christianity was an important part of Medieval life; it was believed the king was appointed by God. The Church was very powerful. Led by the Pope in Rome but controlled in England by bishops and other members of the clergy, the Church owned large amounts of land and set rules on everything from marriage to inheritance.

King John is not always remembered as a good Medieval king as he fell out with the Pope and the barons. The Pope wanted Stephen Langton to be the Archbishop of Canterbury but John wanted someone who would be less loyal to the Pope; he wanted someone who would listen to him instead. The Pope retaliated by cancelling all church services, including marriages and funerals. This made the barons very unhappy as they thought they would go to hell.

John was also not very good in battle, losing vast areas of territory in France that England once ruled over. This earned him the nicknames 'lackland' and 'softsword'. As a result, John struggled to raise enough money to govern and defend the country.

Some people do remember John as a good king due to his religious tolerance and fair justice system.

They were worried about invasions from foreign countries because of the fall out with the Pope; John did not maintain good relations with the Pope

They had to pay **scutage** – a high tax on those barons who did not fight for John when he asked

John's poor battle record meant he lost land in France

The barons were unhappy because …

John repeatedly ignored the demands of the Great Council which meant the barons felt their views were not respected

Barons' dissatisfaction

The barons were fed up with John so they raised an army against him and occupied London. John realised he would need to listen to the barons so met with them on 15 June 1215 to negotiate the way in which the country should be governed.

 **APPLY**

SOURCE ANALYSIS

▶ **SOURCE A** *A picture from a history of France written in 1250. It shows the battle of Bouvines in which King John was defeated. As a result England lost more land in France and King John had to pay the French king, Philip, £40,000 to bring the war to an end and accept a truce*

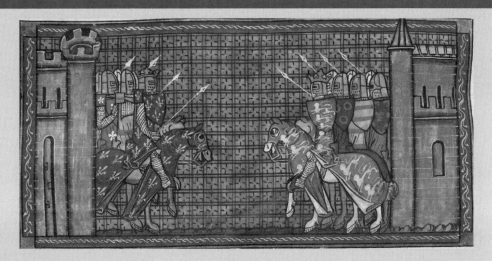

a Complete the following table.

Qualities of a Medieval king	Why these were important
Defend the people by leading the army well	
country peacefull	- war majority unhappy
rebellions	- limit power/king rls supreme
church and pope	- religious beliefs/hell

b Make a list of the successes of King John's reign and another list of his failures.

c **EXAM QUESTION** Study **Source A**. How useful is **Source A** to a historian studying the barons' dissatisfaction with King John's rule?

EXAMINER TIP ⌖

Try to link something you can see in the picture with the provenance and your own knowledge. Use your answers from parts **a** and **b** to help you.

Magna Carta and its impact

The English barons lost patience with King John and were prepared to fight him. Because John needed their support to stay in power, he had to agree to their demands when they met at Runnymede in 1215. It was here that John signed Magna Carta.

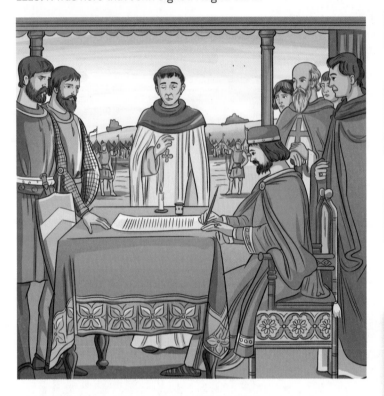

Magna Carta

We grant to all freemen all the liberties written below:

- a baron's heir shall inherit his lands on payment of £100 to the king
- no scutage shall be imposed on the barons except with the common counsel of the realm
- no freeman shall be arrested or imprisoned without a proper trial and according to the law of the land
- the English Church shall be free to make its own appointments
- all merchants shall have safety, in staying and travelling in England, for buying and selling goods, free from evil tolls
- a group of 25 barons will be created to monitor the king and ensure he commits to Magna Carta (Clause 61).

First Barons' War

King John quickly went back on his word, saying he had been forced to sign Magna Carta

The Pope agreed, stating that Magna Carta was invalid

War started in England between the barons and the king; the barons had the support of the French who sent troops and money to help the barons

The **Siege** of Rochester in late 1215 gave John the upper hand after he and his men were able to storm Rochester Castle

How long did it last…?

Timeline:

▼ **May 1216**

- The barons promise the French Prince Louis the English throne, and he arrives on the coast; Prince Louis takes control of most of England, and has the support of the Scottish king

▼ **2 June 1216**

- Prince Louis announced (but not crowned) King of England

▼ **October 1216**

- King John dies

▼ **28 October 1216**

- John's young son Henry becomes King Henry III; Magna Carta reissued and Henry III agrees to the conditions

Magna Carta	
Short term impacts	**Long term impacts**
• King John went back on his word, meaning Magna Carta had no immediate impact on society • Peasants and villeins were still not free; nothing changed for ordinary people at the time • Only the politically powerful such as barons, the Church and merchants benefited from Magna Carta	• Magna Carta introduced the idea that there were some laws and rules the king had to follow • Eventually more people gained their freedom • Kings after John signed similar versions of Magna Carta • It was viewed as the first step in Britain becoming a **democracy**

SUMMARY

- Christian religion was very important in Medieval life, and Medieval kings believed they were appointed by God.

- King John was seen as a bad king as he lost wars, made the barons pay high taxes, and fell out with the Pope.

- John panicked when the barons went against him. He needed their support both in running the country, and in his disagreements with the Pope. At Runnymede in June 1215 the barons made John sign Magna Carta.

- John quickly went back on his word, supported by the Pope.

- The barons gained the support of the French and challenged John again by declaring that the French Prince Louis was king.

- King John died in October 1216 and his young son became King Henry III. Henry agreed to the conditions of Magna Carta.

REVISION SKILLS

Mind-maps or spider diagrams like the one on page 13 can be an excellent way of reviewing information, such as the impacts of Magna Carta. At first, create them to remember specific events or people. You can then make them more concise to include longer periods of time or multiple events. Use colours and small images to make the information memorable.

 **APPLY**

FACTORS

King John's disagreements with his barons were the result of many different factors. Write down one example of each of the following factors relating to King John's disagreements with his barons (one has been completed for you).

- role of the individual
- economy
- government
- religion

Role of the individual: The French Prince Louis had an impact on King John and the barons as Louis' arrival in England showed John how serious the barons were. His presence and desire for the throne helped secure the power of Magna Carta when John's son, Henry, became king.

EXAMINER TIP

This activity can help you plan for an exam question asking you to decide whether, for example, religion was the main factor that caused challenges to royal authority. Note that the Factors exam question will require you to include information about a range of time periods in your answer.

CHAPTER 2

The origins of parliament

 **RECAP**

King Henry III and his barons

When King John died in 1216 his young son became King Henry III and ruled with the help of advisers. In 1234 he started to rule on his own, and before long his relationship with the barons was at breaking point.

The Pope

- Henry III was a very **pious** king which meant he had a close relationship with Pope Innocent IV in Rome. The Pope tried to use Henry to fight wars in Sicily
- Henry was meant to pay the Pope money to fight these wars, and when he did not pay, the new Pope, Alexander IV, threatened to **excommunicate** the king
- The Pope also wanted Henry's brother, Richard, to become Holy Roman Emperor, which was an important job. This meant Henry would feel pressured to help pay for the Pope's wars

The French

- Henry's father, King John, had lost a lot of French lands so Henry had to raise money to fund war campaigns to get them back
- He was unsuccessful at first but then he sent his brother-in-law, the powerful and **aristocratic** Simon de Montfort, who won land back in Gascony and controlled the area for Henry
- Reports reached Henry that Simon de Montfort had been too harsh with the French people so he sent his son, Edward, to keep control

King Henry's problems

The Barons

- By 1254 Henry's relationship with the barons had deteriorated – they were angry about his various schemes
- They were angry that Henry's French family were given jobs in the English court and Italian **clergy** were given top jobs in the Church
- Henry's tax increases to pay the Pope made the barons angry as they were the ones who had to pay

The Provisions of Oxford, 1258

Due to the issues between the barons and the king they refused to support him. Simon de Montfort led the barons to call a Great Council meeting in 1258. Here, King Henry had to agree to the Provisions of Oxford.

The barons also refused to fund the planned payment to the Pope over the wars in Sicily. The Provisions of Oxford gave the barons great power. Barons could now make decisions without the king's approval, but the king could not make decisions without the approval of the council.

The Provisions of Oxford, extended in 1259 in the Provisions of Westminster, reformed local government and gave more power to the less powerful and wealthy in society. This angered some older barons, who felt the reforms were getting in the way of their local interests. Some younger barons were angered by the provisions as they were not elected to the council and therefore lost their influence. The barons were divided.

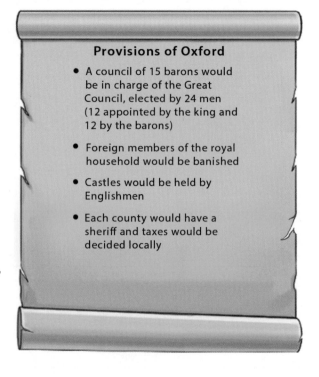

Provisions of Oxford

- A council of 15 barons would be in charge of the Great Council, elected by 24 men (12 appointed by the king and 12 by the barons)
- Foreign members of the royal household would be banished
- Castles would be held by Englishmen
- Each county would have a sheriff and taxes would be decided locally

 APPLY

FACTORS

a Complete the following table, identifying 3–4 factors involved in the creation of the Provisions of Oxford. The first row has been done for you.

Problem with Henry's rule	Factor	How important was it for causing the Provisions of Oxford (on a scale of 1–5)?
Foreign influence	Government – The barons were worried that the king was allowing family members from France to have important jobs; the barons worried the king was being influenced by people who did not have the barons' interests at heart	2 – It is important but it is more of a side issue; tax and relations with the Pope had more of an impact on the barons
Barons		
french land loss		
the pope		

b Use your table to create a mind-map as a plan for answering the question:

> **EXAM QUESTION** Was religion the main factor in the creation of the Provisions of Oxford?

 EXAMINER TIP
When giving a judgement you should show how different events link together.

 REVIEW
Remember that the factors you have been considering in your study of Power and the People include: war, religion, chance, government, communication, economy, ideas such as equality/democracy/representation, the role of individuals. Each event may link to more than one factor.

EXAMINER TIP
Always write about the given factor and then compare it to another two. For Levels 3 and 4 try to compare all the factors in order to give a judgement on which one is the most important.

SIMILARITY

> **EXAM QUESTION** Explain two ways in which Magna Carta and the Provisions of Oxford were similar.

 REVIEW
To help you identify the similarities, use your answers from the Factors activity, and go back over the content of Chapter 1. Think about the impact Magna Carta had.

Second Barons' War

Henry gained the support of those barons who did not like de Montfort and the Provisions of Oxford. Henry wrote to the Pope and asked for his permission to cancel the provisions. In 1261 the Pope agreed, so Henry appointed his own men to the Great Council. Henry was back in charge!

Henry ruled as badly as he had before, and after three years the barons called upon Simon de Montfort. The Second Barons' War began. At the Battle of Lewes in 1264 de Montfort captured the king and imprisoned his son, the young Prince Edward. Simon de Montfort was now in charge and England was on its way to becoming a **republic**.

The Parliament of 1265 and the first 'Commons'

> Simon de Montfort created a council of nine of his closest friends and allies

→

> He reconfirmed Magna Carta and the Provisions of Oxford

↓

> In 1265 de Montfort called a meeting of the Great Council inviting rich merchants (the **burgesses**) and knights: this meant he had now secured support from ordinary people – the burgesses of the towns – who were sometimes referred to as 'commoners'. This group later became known as the Commons, in this early form of **parliament**. This developed democracy in England and would help pave the way for all groups to have a voice.

←

> Barons started to worry that he had become too powerful

The Battle of Evesham, 1265

The barons started to get concerned that de Montfort was becoming an **autocrat** so they put their support behind Henry. Prince Edward had been released from prison and had raised an army. They were out to get de Montfort. On 4 August 1265 at the Battle of Evesham de Montfort fell from his horse. His body was cut into pieces and sent around the country as a warning.

The monarchy was back!

REVISION SKILLS

Reducing information to a shorter, more concise form is valuable. After reading a couple of pages of a textbook or your notes, ask yourself, 'what are the 6 most important things I need to remember?' Write those down on a piece of paper or small card. Do not worry about the things that you have left behind on the page; you will remember those next time!

Significance of the Parliament of 1265

Short term

- Henry III ruled until 1272 but he never called another meeting of the Great Council; when his son Edward became King Edward I he learned from his father's mistakes and called many parliaments
- In 1295 Edward called the **Model Parliament**, which was the first parliament that resembled our parliament today, with invited aristocrats, and elected commoners

Medium term

- The king's power was challenged again in 1649 with the death of Charles I and the start of the English Revolution; a republic governed for a period of time
- The king's power was not totally changed until the Glorious Revolution of 1688 and the 1689 Bill of Rights – parliament gained more control than the monarch

Long term

- 1840s: The Chartists campaigned for representation for the working class
- Women waited a long time for their voices to be heard: all women and men over the age of 21 got the vote in 1928 (from 1918–28 women aged 21–30 were allowed to vote but only if they owned property)

Today

- The queen or king is a figurehead with no direct influence over the government

REVISION SKILLS

This topic is a thematic study, which means you need to understand themes not only within time periods but across them too. Above is an example of how to link different historical periods that you will encounter later in the revision guide. Keep your own timeline from c1170 to the present day to help you keep track of different themes. Use a different colour for different themes, and keep adding to this timeline as you read this revision guide.

SUMMARY

- Henry III started to rule on his own in 1234 and quickly annoyed the barons.
- The Pope threatened to excommunicate Henry unless he funded war with Sicily.
- Simon de Montfort was close to the king and fought for him in France, but then lost favour.
- Henry started to raise taxes to fight the French – de Montfort led the barons against the king.
- De Montfort called a Great Council in 1258, where the king's power was limited by the Provisions of Oxford.
- At the Battle of Lewes in 1264 de Montfort and the barons took full control.
- An early form of a parliament with the burgesses was called in 1265.
- Monarchy was restored along with royal authority after the Battle of Evesham in 1265.
- In 1295 King Edward I held the first Model Parliament.

APPLY

EXPLAIN THE SIGNIFICANCE

a Identify two ways in which Simon de Montfort helped to make Britain more democratic.

b Describe the biggest change from the 1265 parliament to the 1295 parliament for the development of greater democracy.

c List the ways in which the new ideas brought about by Simon de Montfort can still be seen today.

d EXAM QUESTION: Explain the significance of the 1265 parliament.

EXAMINER TIP

For higher level answers you must write about two or more aspects of significance. Use the timeline on this page to help you pick two points. Try to think about change and impact on democracy.

Medieval revolt and royal authority

RECAP

Causes of the Peasants' Revolt

Life for the peasants of Medieval England was hard. They were at the bottom of the feudal system working for a lord and serving the king. In the fourteenth century the peasants had had enough; they decided to fight back.

Economic

- In 1348 the plague or Black Death arrived in England; it killed most of the peasant workforce, so fields of crops were left to rot and villages were abandoned; as there were fewer workers, the peasants could demand higher wages
- King Richard II raised taxes to fund his campaigns against the French in the Hundred Years War – it was called a **poll tax**
- By 1380 everyone over the age of 15 had to pay four **groats** per year to the king; this was a massive increase from the one groat they had previously paid

Political

- Local lords and even the king worried that the peasants were becoming too powerful and that the feudal system would break down
- In 1351 King Edward III passed the Statute of Labourers which restricted the movement and wages of the peasants; they were forced to return and work for their lord again
- The peasants wanted reform to reduce the influence of landowners

Causes of the revolt

Religious

- Many priests started to preach that the Church was exploiting the peasants by making people pay **pardons** for their sins
- John Ball, a priest, said that God had created everyone equally and there should be no rich or poor; Ball was arrested

Social

- The Black Death plague spread across the country killing a third of the population – mostly poor people
- Many peasants started to move around from village to village looking for the best paid work
- Between 1377 and 1379, 70% of the people brought before the **Justice of the Peace** were accused of breaking the Statute of Labourers
- Peasants returning from the Hundred Years War were forced to go back to their old lives and pay higher taxes

The revolt of 1381

Timeline

▼ 30 May
- Peasants refuse to pay poll tax and threaten to kill local tax collector

▼ 2 June
- Chief Justice comes to collect poll tax and is also threatened; peasants find tax collector's clerks and behead them, also set fire to houses of poll tax supporters

▼ 7 June
- Peasants march to Maidstone and make Wat Tyler their leader; they free John Ball, storm Rochester Castle and burn tax records

▼ 12 June
- Peasants reach London's city walls and Richard II sails to meet them, but the crowd is too rowdy

▼ 13 June
- Peasants storm the city walls, burn palaces and kill supporters of the king; some peasants are peaceful as Wat Tyler had ordered

▼ 14 June
- Wat Tyler meets the king and outlines the peasants' demands; the king agrees and asks the peasants to go home. While this is happening, another group of peasants kills the Archbishop of Canterbury

▼ 15 June
- The king meets the peasants again and agrees to their demands, but one of his men kills Wat Tyler; the peasants leave London and the revolt is over

Peasants' demands

- All villeins to be made freemen
- Full change to the system of law
- Church lands to be given to the people
- All bishops except one to be removed

Richard went back on his word. He said he had been forced to agree to the demands so it did not count. The rebel leaders were all rounded up and hanged, and John Ball's and Wat Tyler's heads were stuck on spikes on London Bridge.

APPLY

FACTORS
a Look at the mind-map of the revolt's causes. Put the factors that caused the revolt in order from most important to least important.

b Annotate your list with evidence to support your reasons for deciding on the importance of each factor.

EXAMINER TIP
This activity can help you plan for a 16-mark exam question asking you to decide whether a factor such as economy or religion is the main factor in the causes of challenges to royal authority. Note that the Factors exam question requires you to include information about a range of time periods in your answer.

REVISION SKILLS
Use a map of southeast England to plot where the peasants went from 30 May to 15 June. This will help you to visualise the revolt when answering questions in the exam.

Impact of the Peasants' Revolt

After Wat Tyler's death the peasants disbanded and went home. It is easy to dismiss the Peasants' Revolt as a failure as their leader was killed and King Richard did not change anything, but that is not the whole story.

King Richard did stop the poll tax after the revolt. It was not repeated until 1989 in Scotland and 1990 in England and Wales

The peasants' wages began to rise because the situation before the revolt remained the same: there was a lack of workers so the peasants could demand more money. Parliament eventually gave in and stopped trying to control the peasants' wages. The Statute of Labourers was eventually withdrawn

Some peasants were even able to buy their own land because there was so much unused after the Black Death

Gradually peasants became more independent and within 100 years peasants and villeins were freemen

Some historians believe that the revolt was unnecessary; they say that society was already changing and that serfdom was coming to an end

What do historians think?

Most historians believe that the revolt was significant, as it was the first time ordinary people, or the working class, had rebelled; some historians further believe that the revolt marks the start of English ideas of freedom

SUMMARY

- The Black Death arrived in England in 1348, killing a third of the population.

- There were fewer workers so the peasants started to demand higher wages.

- The Statute of Labourers was passed in 1351 as a way to control the peasants and their rising wages.

- King Richard II was fighting France in the Hundred Years War – he needed funding so he introduced a poll tax.

- John Ball started to preach about how the Church had been exploiting peasants.

- There were uprisings in Essex and Kent against the bad priests and evil landowners.

- Wat Tyler became the leader of the revolt and the peasants marched to London in 1381.

- The king agreed to speak with the rebels but there was too much violence at first. He eventually met with Wat Tyler, and agreed to his demands.

- Wat Tyler was killed on 15 June 1381, possibly by one of the king's men.

- King Richard went back on his word. In the short term, the revolt ended in favour of the king, but it had a lasting impact on land ownership, wages, taxes and freedom.

 APPLY

REVISION SKILLS

Making revision cards is a good way of revising and creating a useful revision aid for later use. Write a heading/topic such as 'The Peasants' Revolt' on the front of each card, and on the back jot down three or four things related to the topic. Try to include a factual detail with each point.

SIMILARITY

a Complete the diagram with the short- and long-term impacts of the Peasants' Revolt.

Short-term	Long-term

b Explain two ways in which the signing of Magna Carta and the Peasants' Revolt were similar.

EXAMINER TIP

You could refer to the causes of each event and their impact both long and short term. Think about which factors were important to both events.

REVIEW

To help you identify the similarities between the two events you should review Chapter 1 on the signing of Magna Carta.

EXAMINER TIP

Make sure you know the question types you will be asked in each part of the exam. Find out how many marks there are for each type of question. For example, this question is worth 8 marks.

CHAPTER 4

Popular uprisings against the Crown

 **RECAP**

Henry VIII and the Reformation

In the sixteenth century the Church was at the centre of communities. Monasteries were places of learning and culture, offered medical treatment, and sometimes acted as refuges for the poor or homeless. People were so worried about going to hell that they paid the Church **indulgences** to be forgiven for their sins and to help them get to heaven

The **Reformation** was a religious movement in the 1500s that began as an attempt to reform the Roman Catholic Church because of:

- the Church's wealth
- the Church's influence in society.

These ideas were fuelled by the writings of Martin Luther in 1517. He translated the Bible into German and criticised the Church for selling indulgences.

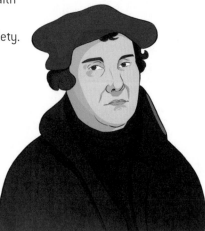

Martin Luther

Henry made himself head of the Church of England in 1534 with the **Act of Supremacy**. He did this with the help of his adviser, Thomas Cromwell. Cromwell was a blacksmith's son who was well travelled. He helped Henry divorce Catherine of Aragon and increase his wealth.

Thomas Cromwell

> **Why did King Henry VIII support the Reformation?**
>
> | | | |
> |---|---|---|
> | Henry saw the Pope as a competing power; he wanted the people of England to listen to him only | Henry wanted a divorce from Catherine of Aragon but the Pope would not allow it | If Henry was in charge of the Church himself, he would not need to pay the Pope taxes |

The monasteries

Thomas Cromwell promised to make Henry VIII the richest king in Europe and to do it he would take the wealth from the monasteries.

- The Church had an annual income of more than £200,000 which meant it earned nearly double that of the king – Henry wanted this wealth.
- Small monasteries with an annual income of less than £200 were shut down in 1536.
- *Valor Ecclesiasticus* was set up by Cromwell to evaluate the monasteries: he had reports written about how the monasteries were spending their money. If they were not being run properly they were shut down. Those writing the reports were encouraged to make the monasteries sound worse than they were, making it easier to close them.

Henry needed to make money and closing the monasteries was, in his eyes, the obvious choice. Not everyone was happy about him taking so much control.

Causes of the Pilgrimage of Grace

Rising prices

Prices continued to rise under Henry; his advisers were blamed

Why were people unhappy about Henry's changes?

Changes to religion

Many people wanted the monasteries back, with the Pope as the head of the Church

Landowners lost influence

Those who had been supporters of Catherine of Aragon fell out of favour after the divorce

Cromwell's power

Cromwell was hated by landowners who resented his influence; he was blamed for the changes to the Church

In 1536 a rebellion broke out in Yorkshire by devout Christians who were angry about the changes to the Church. They had the following demands:

- restore the monasteries because of their importance within the community
- recognise the Pope as the head of the Church
- dismiss Cromwell and other ministers who were giving the king poor advice.

This rebellion was known as the Pilgrimage of Grace.

REVISION SKILLS

Break down the information about a topic in different ways. You could create a brief fact file, containing two or three important points about the country, person or event concerned.

⚙ APPLY

FACTORS

a Why was Martin Luther upset with the Catholic Church?

b Write a brief description of the actions of Henry VIII when dealing with the Church.

c Create a timeline of key dates and events leading up to the Pilgrimage of Grace.

d Write down an example of how each of the following led to the Pilgrimage of Grace.

- role of the individual
- religion
- economy
- government

EXAMINER TIP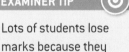

Lots of students lose marks because they simply describe what happened, rather than explaining factors. This activity will help you to develop the skill of explaining the factors.

REVISION SKILLS

Memory maps or spider diagrams can be an excellent way of reviewing and organising information. Use colours and small images to make the information memorable.

 **RECAP**

Implications for royal authority

King Henry VIII was in no doubt about the purpose of the Pilgrimage of Grace. The marchers carried a banner showing the five wounds of Christ. This uprising was about religion and against the king's advisers, who were seen to be corrupting it.

The rebels had found a leader in a lawyer called Robert Aske. He was able to put the case together to show that the pilgrims were not against the king himself and had no intention of challenging royal authority.

Actions of the 'rebels'

Throughout October 1536 the pilgrims captured key locations.

The Duke of Norfolk had been selected by Henry to negotiate with the pilgrims as he

- was a Catholic
- was a strong critic of Cromwell.

Norfolk agreed to take the new list of demands from the pilgrims to Henry. They were the same as before but they added that a parliament must meet in York to provide better representation for the north.

1 They started in Lincoln with Lord Hussey who had supported Catherine of Aragon; he wanted a removal of tax in peacetime

2 The town of York and Pontefract Castle were captured; they had been held by Lord Darcy but he surrendered and joined the pilgrims

4 On 27 October the Duke of Norfolk met the pilgrims at Doncaster Bridge; he had an army of 8000 men, and Aske had 30,000

3 By the end of October, they had control of most of England north of Cheshire and Lincolnshire

REVIEW ↻

Look back at page 25 to remind yourself what the pilgrims' original demands were.

Aske and Henry

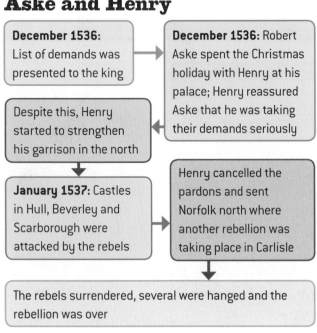

December 1536: List of demands was presented to the king

December 1536: Robert Aske spent the Christmas holiday with Henry at his palace; Henry reassured Aske that he was taking their demands seriously

Despite this, Henry started to strengthen his garrison in the north

January 1537: Castles in Hull, Beverley and Scarborough were attacked by the rebels

Henry cancelled the pardons and sent Norfolk north where another rebellion was taking place in Carlisle

The rebels surrendered, several were hanged and the rebellion was over

Impact of the uprising

Impacts of the Pilgrimage of Grace		
Religious	**Economic**	**Political**
• Failed to stop dissolution of the monasteries • In 1539 many larger monasteries were dissolved	• The economy improved with the money from the monasteries and Henry was able to develop the Royal Navy • Landowners bought the monastery land	• Cromwell had Darcy, Hussey and Aske killed • Henry strengthened the Council of the North • No more rebellions took place during Henry's reign • Cromwell eventually fell out of Henry's favour and was executed in 1540

SUMMARY

- In 1517 Martin Luther published his writings that were critical of the Roman Catholic Church.

- Henry VIII sought a divorce from Catherine of Aragon.

- In 1524 the Act of Supremacy saw the creation of the Church of England.

- In 1536 Thomas Cromwell started the dissolution of the monasteries as a way to get more money for the king.

- Both landowners and commoners were distressed by the dissolution and started the Pilgrimage of Grace.

- Henry squashed the rebellion and killed the leaders.

- The Pilgrimage of Grace was a failure and Henry saw no more rebellions for the rest of his reign.

 **APPLY**

EXPLAIN THE SIGNIFICANCE

a In what ways did the Pilgrimage of Grace make an impact on Henry's policies?

b In your opinion, what was the biggest impact? Explain your choice.

c   EXAM QUESTION — Explain the significance of the Pilgrimage of Grace.

EXAMINER TIP

Make sure you refer to different types of impact, such as political and economic, as well as some longer-term results.

SOURCE ANALYSIS

▶ **SOURCE A** *A woodcut illustration showing Henry VIII sitting on the throne with the Pope (Clement) being used as a footstool. Henry has a sword in his hand and a Bible in his lap. This woodcutting was created in 1534 for John Foxe's 'Actes and Monumentes'. Foxe was a Catholic who wrote about Protestant* **martyrs**

EXAM QUESTION — Study **Source A**. How useful is **Source A** to a historian studying Henry VIII and the Pilgrimage of Grace?

EXAMINER TIP

Remember to refer to the causes of the Pilgrimage of Grace when looking at the source content.

RECAP

Causes of the English Revolution

Charles I became king in 1625 after his father James I (James VI of Scotland) died. Many historians believe that James had been a good king in regard to religion but he had caused tension with parliament because he was an extravagant king who liked to give money to his friends. Parliament would not let Charles make the mistakes his father had. Within 20 years of becoming king, Charles would be at war with his own country and would eventually have his head chopped off. This sequence of events is called the English Revolution. Why did it happen?

English Revolution: main causes

Charles I believed that kings derived their authority from God, so should not have to justify their actions to any earthly authority such as a parliament; this was known as the **divine right** of kings		A new prayer book in 1637 upset the Scots so much they gathered an army	
The king had **favourites**, such as the Duke of Buckingham		The Scots defeated Charles' army, then invaded England	
Charles ruled without parliament from 1629		**Puritans** wrote critically and were punished by the **Star Chamber**	
The king taxed everybody with Ship Money in 1637		The Short Parliament, April 1640, would not give Charles money to fight the Scots	
Charles married a French Catholic, Henrietta Maria		Parliament worried that the Earl of Strafford would help Charles rule England with an Irish army	
The Church became more Catholic with the changes introduced by Archbishop William Laud			

After the **Laudian** reforms (those introduced by William Laud) imposed a new prayer book in Scotland, some Presbyterians in Scotland joined together and signed an agreement called a **covenant** in 1638. The covenant said they would not accept the changes. Those who signed the agreement and their supporters became known as Covenanters.

Summary of the causes of the English Revolution

- Parliament did not trust King Charles I because of his religious links and his attempts to rule the country without consulting parliament on matters of finance, religion and foreign policy.
- Charles wanted to rule the country without having to consult parliament.

 APPLY

FACTORS

In the exam you may get a factors question that asks you the main causes of challenges to royal authority or the main causes of increased parliamentary authority. Start thinking about how you would answer this kind of question by categorising each of the events in the table on page 28. Next to each event, draw a symbol or symbols to represent what type of factor(s) it is. Choose from the following (two have been done for you in the table already):

government   religion   war

the economy   role of the individual

REVISION SKILLS

Why not draw to help you revise? Use sketches, doodles and pictures to help make facts memorable. You do not have to be a good artist to do this!

SOURCE ANALYSIS

◀ **SOURCE A**

A woodcut from c1638–42 of the Scottish Covenanters petitioning Charles I. The Covenanters are holding a copy of the new prayer book which was imposed by William Laud

EXAMINER TIP

You should spend about ten minutes on the source question. Plan your time carefully in the exam – make sure you leave enough time for the longer essay questions.

a Describe the changes Charles made to religion.

b Why were some Scottish Presbyterians so upset about the changes to religion?

c Why might the Covenanters be showing Charles I a copy of the prayer book?

d How would you describe the way Charles has been portrayed in the woodcut?

e **EXAM QUESTION** Study **Source A**. How useful is **Source A** to a historian studying the causes of the English Revolution?

EXAMINER TIP

To obtain a higher level, link what you can see in the source to your own knowledge.

The Civil War: who fought whom?

The Civil War started in Nottingham in August 1642. Charles I declared war on parliament, and called on all his supporters for help. However, not everyone was a loyal supporter of the king.

Cavaliers (royalists)

- Wealthy landowners who did not want to lose their wealth
- Mainly based in northern England
- Those who were worried about the growing influence of parliament

Roundheads (parliamentarians)

- Supported by middle-class and peasant workers
- Mainly based in southern England and London
- Mostly merchants who were not happy about the king's taxes
- Those who did not support Charles' religious and political reforms

Oliver Cromwell

- MP for Cornwall
- Led parliamentary forces with Thomas Fairfax
- Created New Model Army
- A Puritan

New Model Army

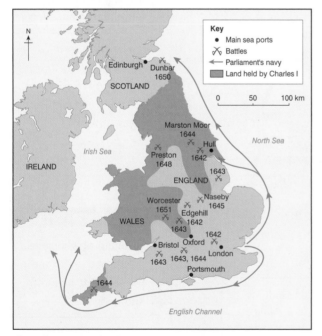

Key
- ● Main sea ports
- ✗ Battles
- ← Parliament's navy
- ▨ Land held by Charles I

0   50   100 km

▲ The land held by Charles I and key battles of the English Civil War

The war had started with no clear winner at the Battle of Edgehill, 1642. The king then tried to take London but failed, and withdrew to Oxford. Both sides had fought using **cavalry** and **infantry**, and used tactics that had been seen in many battles before.

Most parliamentarians did not want the full removal of the king, they simply wanted a removal of royal reforms. Cromwell on the other hand was angry about this, and was committed to removing the king. He planned to do this by using his New Model Army.

- He recruited men based on their ability rather than their privilege.
- The army was disciplined and lived by a strict religious and moral code.
- The men were not allowed to drink or swear.

The New Model Army was used for the first time at the Battle of Naseby in 1645, where it was victorious over the king's smaller army. This victory is considered a turning point in the war.	
Statistics	New Model Army: 14,000 men
	(Royalist army: 9000 men)
Tactics	Approached slowly rather than charging
	Manoeuvred behind the royalist infantry and attacked from the rear
Outcome	End of the king's last great army
	The New Model Army went on to capture Bristol and Oxford

The Second Civil War

- 1647: Charles surrendered to the Scottish army which later handed him over to the New Model Army to go on trial for treason.
- However, while negotiating with parliament, Charles encouraged a Scottish army to invade England and make the English Church Presbyterian.
- 1648: At the Battle of Preston the Scots fought the New Model Army. The Scots were defeated and Charles confirmed that he could not be trusted.
- December 1648: The regiment of Thomas Pride surrounded parliament. They refused entry to those who supported the king (Pride's **Purge**). Charles would be tried with no one to support him.

Many parliamentarians were not happy that Charles continued to challenge the authority of government and limit the development of democracy. This would go against him during his trial.

APPLY

FACTORS

a Construct a spider diagram to show all the events involved in the English Civil War between 1642 and 1648. Use two colours to highlight royalist and parliamentarian facts.

b Describe Oliver Cromwell's aims.

c What was new about the New Model Army?

EXAMINER TIP

Another factor to explain Charles' defeat could be the role of the individual. You could write about either Oliver Cromwell or Thomas Pride.

EXAMINER TIP

The New Model Army during the English Civil War would be good content to use when explaining 'war' as a factor. You should think about how the New Model Army helped to defeat Charles.

REVIEW

Go back and look at pages 14–15 and 18–19 to see how the First and Second Barons' Wars contribute to war as a factor for challenging royal authority and developing greater democracy.

The trial of Charles I

In January 1649 King Charles I was put on trial, charged with treason. Of the 135 **commissioners** that were due to turn up, only 68 were present. There was a feeling that things had gone too far — remember, most people had wanted to remove royal reforms, not the king himself. One person who was sure the king had to go was Oliver Cromwell.

- On 27 January 1649 King Charles was found guilty of treason and sentenced to death. The court president justified this by saying Charles had attacked the basic liberties of the country by refusing to call parliament.
- On 30 January 1649 the king was beheaded. Charles had to wait hours until they found an executioner who was willing to kill him. Furthermore, they needed to pass a law that stopped a new monarch being installed on the king's death.

Justifications for the king's execution

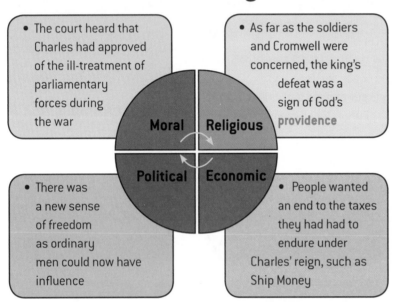

- The court heard that Charles had approved of the ill-treatment of parliamentary forces during the war

- As far as the soldiers and Cromwell were concerned, the king's defeat was a sign of God's providence

Moral | Religious | Political | Economic

- There was a new sense of freedom as ordinary men could now have influence

- People wanted an end to the taxes they had had to endure under Charles' reign, such as Ship Money

After the execution

After Charles I's execution Oliver Cromwell became the leader of the Commonwealth. A 'commonwealth' is a term for a political community founded for the common good. The new commonwealth would be a republic.

REVISION SKILLS

Identify keywords in a passage. Write out the keywords. Give someone the passage. Using only the keywords can you explain to them what the passage was about?

Impact on the Commonwealth of the English Revolution and Charles' execution

New ideas	• The Levellers were a politically radical group who spread the idea of votes for all men and a more equal society
	• The Diggers were similar to the Levellers but they campaigned for land reform
	• English society changed to become more equal and ordered because of Puritanism
Religion	• Cromwell was a Puritan and wanted society to reflect his beliefs
	• However, people were free to worship however they liked
	• Jews, who had been banished from England in 1290, were invited back into Britain
	• Religious radicalism developed
Economy	• The Navigation Act of 1651 stated that only English ships could arrive at or leave England
	• The system of taxation was reorganised to make it more efficient for everyone
Politics	• Cromwell won wars against the Spanish and Dutch, restoring England's reputation abroad
	• He appointed Major Generals to the 11 districts he created — they kept strict control over everyone

In 1660 Charles' son became king, as Charles II. There were limits to what he could do and parliament had much more power. In 1689 a law was passed completely limiting the powers of the king.

Cromwell and the Commonwealth

Cromwell is one of the most disputed figures in history. Opinions of him changed depending on political events:

- In the 1660s, during the time of the restoration of the monarchy under Charles II, many people saw Cromwell as the devil.
- In the nineteenth century, when Britain was moving more towards a democracy and parliament was more important, historians were kinder to Cromwell.

SUMMARY

- King Charles I believed in the divine right of kings.
- Parliament was sent away for 11 years and Charles ruled on his own.
- Charles made everyone pay Ship Money.
- Many people were angry about the religious reforms Charles imposed.
- Parliament was called twice in 1640 to raise funds to fight the Scots.
- Oliver Cromwell and the New Model Army defeated the king and his supporters.
- The king was executed and Britain became a republic.

REVISION SKILLS

The English Civil War introduced new ideas about royal authority. Keep notes where you can see these ideas as you revise the rest of the course.

REVIEW

Look back at pages 28–31 to review all the events of the English Revolution.

⚙ APPLY

EXPLAIN THE SIGNIFICANCE

a List the reasons why people were annoyed with royal authority during the reign of Charles I.

b Describe the reasons for the execution of Charles I.

c Copy and complete the table to compare the rule of Charles I with the period after the English Civil War.

	Charles I	After Civil War
Economy		
Religion		
Politics		

d Explain the significance of the English Revolution.

EXAMINER TIP

Make sure you refer to different types of impact, such as political and economic impacts, as well as some longer-term results. For full marks try to show how the significance has changed over different periods.

EXAMINER TIP

In order to achieve a higher lever here you would have to mention where ideas of challenging royal authority can be seen later in the course, such as in the American Revolution. For higher marks, try to show how events can have a different or new significance with the passing of time as people may change what they see as important in history.

CHAPTER 6

Royal authority and the right to representation

 RECAP

During the seventeenth century Britain had become very powerful. It took over other parts of the world, including large parts of North America. However, by the 1760s–70s the people of America were unhappy about being part of the British **Empire**.

- Britain used North America as a **colony** to grow crops like cotton, tobacco and sugar.

- The British also used North America as a **penal colony**. Around 50,000 British convicts were sent to colonial America.
- By the early 1700s there were 13 separate English colonies in North America and by 1775 there were around 2.5 million settlers. Many became wealthy by dealing in slaves.

Causes of the American Revolution

Long term

- Americans resented paying for the British army's presence in North America.
- Navigation Acts (passed in the mid-1600s, but still in force) meant that the colonists could only trade with Britain, not other countries.
- Colonists disagreed with land boundaries that the British had agreed with the Native Americans.

Medium term

- The Americans were ruled from Britain yet they had no representatives in the British parliament.
- Stamp Tax – a tax on all documents including newspapers – was very unpopular.
- They were unhappy at paying taxes without having a say in them. They used the slogan: 'No taxation without representation!'

Short term

- 1770 Boston Massacre – the British army shot and killed some anti-British colonists.
- 1773 Boston Tea Party – colonists poured British tea into the harbour in protest at the Tea Tax imposed by the British.
- 1775 Lexington incident – British soldiers were fired on when they tried to seize some gunpowder. This was the start of the American Revolution.

The Declaration of Independence

The Americans met in **Congress** to decide what to do about the British. By 1775 George Washington had become the leader of their army.

A Declaration of Independence was issued in 1776 in Philadelphia. It stated that the 13 colonies were free and that all control from Britain had ended. Seven years of fighting followed to achieve this.

Turning point: Yorktown

- The decisive battle of the war was at Yorktown in 1781.
- The Americans had 3000 extra men and they had the support of the French.
- The French had secured the waters around Yorktown so the British could not get their supplies in from the sea.
- British troops moved onto a peninsula as they awaited supplies.
- George Washington attacked the British. The British were forced to surrender.

British royal authority had been successfully challenged by a group who had a clear cause: the development of democracy.

Impact and significance of the American Revolution

Consequences for America

- Set up their own system of government with a **constitution**, Congress and a President
- The system still exists today
- Poor people didn't get the vote despite the Declaration of Independence stating that 'all men are created equal'
- Slavery still existed and Native Americans were still discriminated against
- By the early twentieth century America had developed into the most powerful country in the world

Consequences for Britain

- Relations with France worsened after the war, because of French support for the Americans
- Britain used Australia and New Zealand as new penal colonies
- India became the most important colony – the 'jewel in the crown'
- Britain had to deal with its growing working-class population who might like the idea of overthrowing authority

Consequences for the world

- The American Revolution inspired the French Revolution and King Louis XVI was executed
- The French Revolution inspired the working class in Britain and other countries to demand voting rights and better representation

SUMMARY

- America was part of Britain's empire.
- The British imposed taxes on the colonists as a way to make money.
- The colonists were angry that they had no representation in the British government.
- British control in America was resisted and the American Revolution began.
- Britain lost control of America after the Battle of Yorktown.
- America became an independent country with its own constitution.

APPLY

FACTORS

a Make flashcards for the short- and long-term causes of the American Revolution.

b Highlight the cards to show the following factors (a different colour for each).

- economy
- politics

c

> **EXAM QUESTION** Was the main factor that caused the American Revolution political? Explain your answer with reference to political causes and other factors.

EXAMINER TIP

Write one paragraph about political reasons, then another about economic reasons and finally, in a conclusion, show how they interacted.

REVISION SKILLS

Repetition is vital for good long-term memory. Plan revision sessions in short bursts of 20 to 30 minutes several times a day.

CHAPTER 7

The extension of the franchise

RECAP

Problems with Britain's electoral system

In the nineteenth century, the working class grew in size due to the Industrial Revolution. They demanded representation. This challenge to the authority of those with influence and the demand for democracy would change Britain forever.

```
The king and the
major landowners
controlled the country

The workers in the new
towns and cities had no
political representation

Rotten boroughs had no one
living there but still sent two MPs
to parliament

                    Electoral system in the         Pocket boroughs
                    early nineteenth century         were controlled by
                                                     rich individuals

There was no standard property
qualification that gave someone
the right to vote; this meant that
in some places people could
vote if they had a fireplace and
a door with a lock (potwalloper
boroughs) but in others people
had to own a house

No secret ballot meant voters      Women did not have
could be bribed or intimidated     the vote
as everyone knew who they
were voting for
```

The Peterloo Massacre

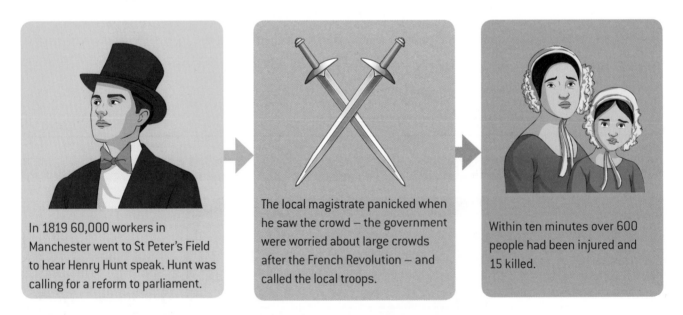

In 1819 60,000 workers in Manchester went to St Peter's Field to hear Henry Hunt speak. Hunt was calling for a reform to parliament.

The local magistrate panicked when he saw the crowd – the government were worried about large crowds after the French Revolution – and called the local troops.

Within ten minutes over 600 people had been injured and 15 killed.

Hunt was arrested and put in prison. After Peterloo the Six Acts were introduced. They stated that any meeting of more than 50 people for radical reform was an act of treason.

New ways to get reform

The working and middle classes still needed change. They decided that instead of protesting they would try to persuade the government to change things and extend the franchise.

There were some important steps in trying to persuade the government:

- Thomas Attwood from Birmingham formed the Birmingham Political Union of the Lower and Middle Classes of People in 1829.
- Attwood, along with 8000 others, sent a **petition** to parliament for reform.
- They wanted: shorter parliaments (to make it harder to buy votes), the end of property qualifications, and the vote for all men who contributed taxes.
- The union was renamed the Birmingham Political Union (BPU) and vowed to cooperate with the law.

The BPU was copied across the country. When Attwood called for people not to pay their taxes the king and government were worried.

The Great Reform Act, 1832

In the 1830 election, the **Tory** party was replaced by the **Whig** party led by Earl Grey. In the same year King George III died and was succeeded by William IV. Both the Whigs and William IV were more progressive and open to reform.

↓

Earl Grey tried three times to pass laws for a reform act but the House of Lords would not pass it. They did not want ordinary people to have more power by being represented in parliament.

↓

On the third attempt Earl Grey requested that the king appoint more lords who were Whigs or sympathetic to reform. Scared that they would lose power and influence, the Tory lords passed the Great Reform Act.

Great Reform Act: main points

- 56 very small locations lose the right to elect their own MPs
- 30 other smaller towns lose one MP
- London and other large towns and cities are given more MPs
- People who earn over £150 per year can vote
- Voters increase from 435,000 to 642,000

How 'great' was the Great Reform Act?

Group	The Great Reform Act
Middle class	• Merchants and industrialists gained more representation • Rotten boroughs were removed and new towns and cities got an MP
Working class	• Most working-class people didn't earn enough to vote • No secret ballot meant those who could vote had to vote for their factory owner/landowner

The Great Reform Act did reduce the power of the king and landowners and proved that change was possible.

 **APPLY**

SIMILARITY

a List the methods used by the campaigners to try to reform parliament.

b Make profiles of the key people or organisations involved as campaigners and in government.

c Write a paragraph giving your judgement about how 'great' the Great Reform Act was.

d **EXAM QUESTION** Explain two ways in which the American colonists and early nineteenth-century parliamentary reformers were similar.

↑

EXAMINER TIP

Identify the similarities first, and then write about the evidence for them specifically, from both topics. Try to find two points of similarity.

REVIEW

You should read Chapter 6 again and repeat activities **a** and **b** for that period to help you answer the exam question.

The causes of Chartism

Working-class men had supported the campaign for reform in 1832. However, even after the Great Reform Act they did not own property worth at least £10, so they did not get the vote. Through their anger, the Chartist movement was born.

Social

- Most workers in the new towns and cities lived in poor conditions
- Bad harvests in the 1830s meant many farmworkers couldn't feed their families

Economic

- Skilled workers were no longer needed because of new machines in factories
- The Poor Law of 1834 sent people with financial problems to the **workhouse**

Causes of Chartism

Political

- The Great Reform Act did not give the working class the vote
- There was still no secret ballot

In 1836 the Chartist movement was born when William Lovett, from the London Working Men's Association, started a campaign with the support of Thomas Attwood and the BPU. The Chartists wanted MPs to be paid because then the working class could become MPs and represent working people in parliament.

Moral or physical force?

	Moral force	Physical force
Leader	William Lovett	Feargus O'Connor
Actions	• Sent first petition to parliament in 1839 **REJECTED** • Sent second petition to parliament in 1842 **REJECTED** • Encouraged **temperance** among members to show they were disciplined and worthy of the vote • Edited a newspaper, *The Chartist*	• Called for violence after the rejection of the 1842 petition • Encouraged workers to damage machinery (plug plot) • Called for a **general strike** and a republic • Sent third petition to parliament in 1848 after return of economic and agricultural depression in 1847 **REJECTED** • Established the more radical newspaper, *Northern Star*

The government was worried about the Chartists so it:

- rejected petitions
- put up posters asking people not to attend Chartist meetings
- arrested Chartists regularly
- transported Chartists to countries like Australia.

Case Study: Newport Rising 1839

- Unemployment was higher than the national average
- Many people were starving
- Protesters planned to release their leader from prison
- Soldiers guarding the prison opened fire and 22 men were killed

The Third Petition, 1848

O'Connor and fewer than 50,000 supporters met on Kennington Common in London on 10 April 1848. The authorities had expected more, so had prepared troops and thousands of police to stop O'Connor's supporters entering the city.

O'Connor had to take the petition into London himself. It was said to have 5 million signatures but it actually only had 2 million and many of the names were forged – including Queen Victoria's name.

The government saw the whole thing as a farce.

The impact of Chartism

Chartism failed in the short term for many reasons:

- strong parliamentary opposition
- standard of living started to increase during the 1850s
- alternative working class movements grew
- divided leadership of Lovett and O'Connor
- lacked one clear message.

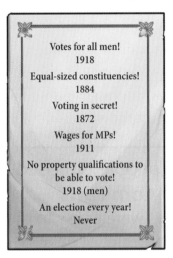

Votes for all men!
1918

Equal-sized constituencies!
1884

Voting in secret!
1872

Wages for MPs!
1911

No property qualifications to
be able to vote!
1918 (men)

An election every year!
Never

◄ *Chartist aims and
the dates they were met*

However, in the long term campaigns for electoral reform were very successful, achieving five of the Chartists' six main aims by 1928.

REVISION SKILLS

Create a quiz about the Chartists and use it to revise with a friend.

SUMMARY

- Britain had a growing working and middle class because of the Industrial Revolution.
- They wanted electoral reform and the vote.
- The government reacted badly when workers gathered at St Peter's Field.
- Earl Grey passed the Great Reform Act 1832 which favoured the middle class.
- The Chartist movement developed to try and get the vote for all men.
- Electoral reform was achieved in the long term.

APPLY

SOURCE ANALYSIS

a Create a mind-map with two arms, one for William Lovett and another for Feargus O'Connor. Add to it showing the different methods used by each. Use colours and small images to make the information memorable.

b Describe the government response to the Chartists.

c Create a timeline containing the key events in the Chartist movement.

d Describe in your own words what is happening in the cartoon in Source A.

e **EXAM QUESTION** Study **Source A**. How useful is **Source A** to a historian studying the failure of Chartism?

▼ **SOURCE A** *A sketch called 'The beginning and the end' published in 1849. It is by John Leech and was published in* Punch, *a humorous and critical magazine*

No. IX.—THE BEGINNING AND THE END.

EXAMINER TIP

Start with picking out what you can see in the cartoon. Then think about what that is trying to say about Chartism and why it failed.

Protest and change

CHAPTER 8

📖 RECAP

The nineteenth century was a time of reform of the working and social lives of those in the new towns and cities. One of the reform movements was the Anti-Corn Law League.

The Corn Laws had been introduced in 1815 because:

- during the war with France, Britain banned cheap French wheat used to make flour for bread
- without any competition, British farmers got a high price for the wheat they grew
- when the war ended many politicians (who were also wealthy landowners) wanted to keep big profits from high wheat prices.

So the Corn Laws kept the price of wheat high, by banning cheap non-British wheat. This made farmers and landowners happy.

Anti-Corn Law League

There were riots across the country as the price of bread increased as a result of the Corn Laws. The working people were not happy.

The Anti-Corn Law League was created and was mostly made up of middle-class men who felt the price controls on wheat were unfair to the poor.

The League had two prominent members:

- Richard Cobden
- Became an MP in 1841

- John Bright
- Became an MP in 1843

> **Reasons people opposed the Corn Laws**
> - Corn Laws were unfair to the poor as the price of basic food – bread – was far too high
> - Cheap wheat could lower living costs
> - People would have more money to spend on other goods, like meat
> - People could buy industrial goods
> - Improved trade with other countries would help to secure peace

Both men were excellent **orators** and spread the word of the League throughout the country. They used the following tactics:

- gave speeches
- created pamphlets
- published newspaper articles
- used the railways to travel faster
- sent pamphlets through the penny post to **reach** every eligible voter.

The new Prime Minister, Robert Peel, saw the benefit of **free trade** and of not controlling imports. He therefore supported the Anti-Corn Law League. However, he was the leader of the Conservative Party, whose members were mostly wealthy landowners who wanted to keep prices high. Peel would need to move slowly to persuade the government.

The Irish Famine

The Irish relied heavily on bread and potatoes for their diet, but in the early 1840s the potato harvest failed. By 1846 Ireland was facing a terrible famine and there was no spare wheat in Britain to send to the millions that were starving. At the same time a crop failure in Scotland and England was threatening the same crisis. Robert Peel's hand was forced; he would need to **repeal** the Corn Laws and allow cheaper foreign wheat to be used to feed the people.

Repeal

Robert Peel repealed the Corn Laws in 1846. He faced so much opposition from his party that he was forced to resign.

British farmers and landowners actually did well even after repeal as the population increased just as the price of wheat was lowered. This gave people more money to spend on barley, oats and meat.

 APPLY

SOURCE ANALYSIS

▶ **SOURCE A** *A cartoon from* Punch *of 1845 showing Robert Peel being taken for a walk by Richard Cobden, one of the leaders of the Anti-Corn Law League. The caption reads:*

'Papa Cobden – Come along, Master Robert, do step out.

Master Robert – That's all very well but you know I cannot go as fast as you do.'

a Briefly describe the reasons the Corn Laws were introduced.

b Make revision cards about the Anti-Corn Law League. Use the following headings: aims, motivations, tactics and outcomes.

c What was Peel's attitude to the Corn Laws?

d Peel was the leader of the Conservative Party. Why did this cause a problem when trying to abolish the Corn Laws?

e **EXAM QUESTION** Study **Source A**. How useful is **Source A** to a historian studying the campaign to repeal the Corn Laws?

PAPA COBDEN TAKING MASTER ROBERT A FREE TRADE WALK.

EXAMINER TIP

For Level 4 think about the purpose of the source. Why has Peel been made to look like a small child? Does that make you think a certain way about Peel?

REVISION SKILLS

Create a 10-point fact test to test detailed knowledge about a topic. You can swap the test with a friend.

The slave trade

Since the 1500s, Britain had been making vast sums of money from the slave trade. The conditions on slave ships and plantations were terrible. A third of slaves died on the ships. If they did survive the journey their life expectancy was only 27.

Abolition movement

Many people in parliament supported slavery, mostly because they made money from the plantations. However, in the late eighteenth century people started to accept it was wrong. The main reasons for this were:

- the comparison to working conditions in factories for so-called 'white slaves'
- religious belief that slavery was not Christian.

One person who held these views was William Wilberforce. He and some like-minded individuals created the Anti-Slavery Society.

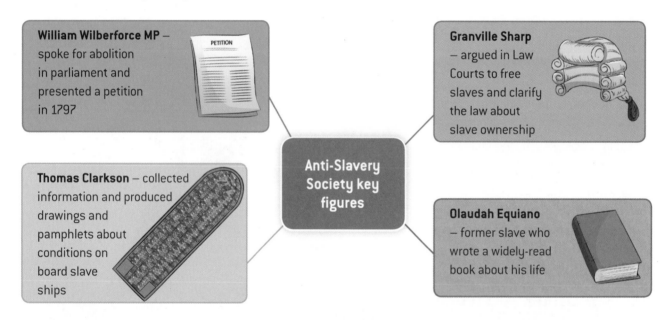

William Wilberforce MP – spoke for abolition in parliament and presented a petition in 1797

PETITION

Granville Sharp – argued in Law Courts to free slaves and clarify the law about slave ownership

Thomas Clarkson – collected information and produced drawings and pamphlets about conditions on board slave ships

Anti-Slavery Society key figures

Olaudah Equiano – former slave who wrote a widely-read book about his life

There were many other important individuals who helped gain support for abolition, such as Hannah More, who wrote poems for the movement, and Josiah Wedgwood, who made a badge for supporters to wear.

Slave resistance

It was not just middle-class white people in Britain who helped bring about the abolition of slavery. There were many instances of slave rebellions.

- The Maroon slaves escaped from their plantation in Jamaica in 1655; they lived in the mountains and celebrated their native African culture.
- Inspired by the French Revolution, the slaves of St Dominique rebelled, killing the white plantation owners and burning the sugar crops; they were victorious – slavery was abolished on the island in 1804.
- The slave rebellions sent the message that slaves were no longer willing to accept slavery, and would use any means necessary to gain freedom.

REVISION SKILLS

When comparing events you could think about CAMO: causes, aims, methods, outcomes.

Comparison of abolition movement and Anti-Corn Law League

Similarities between the movements are shown in **blue**.

Abolition movement		Anti-Corn Law League
• End the slave trade and ownership of slaves	**Aims**	• Repeal the Corn Laws that had been introduced in 1815
• Religion – conviction that slavery was not Christian • Moral	**Motivation**	• Economic – wanted free trade • Social – people were starving
• 1807: Abolished slave trade • 1833: Abolition of Slavery Act – slave ownership banned	**Key dates**	• 1815: Corn Laws introduced • 1846: Famine in Ireland • 1846: Repeal of the Corn Laws
• The middle class • William Wilberforce MP • Factory workers fighting for better conditions	**Supporters**	• The middle class • Robert Peel – prime minister
• Petitions • Speeches in parliament • Arguing for changes in the law • Pamphlets • Public meetings • Books describing the slave experience • Poetry	**Methods**	• Gave speeches • Created pamphlets • Published newspaper articles • Used the railway to travel faster • Sent pamphlets through the penny post to reach every voter
• Many MPs did not support the abolition of the slavery as they were part of the landowning class who made money from slavery	**Reaction**	• Many MPs did not support the repeal of the Corn Laws as they were landowners who made money from the expensive British wheat
• 1833 Act only instantly freed those under the age of six; others not freed for four more years • Slaves were now forced to compete for paid work; they still had to live and work in horrible conditions • Smuggling became widespread and was not regulated	**Impact**	• Robert Peel resigned as prime minister • Farmers and landowners did well after the Corn Laws were repealed • People had more income and could buy expensive goods such as meat • The influence of the landowning class was challenged

 APPLY

SIMILARITY

a Why did people join the abolition movement?

b What tactics did the Anti-Slavery Society use? Create a mind-map to show these.

c Explain two ways in which the abolition movement and the Anti-Corn Law League were similar.

 EXAMINER TIP

Remember that in this particular question you are being asked about similarities – so don't spend time writing about how the two movements were different.

REVIEW

Look at pages 40–41 to remind yourself about the Anti-Corn Law League.

Factory and social reform

The Industrial Revolution started around 1750 and saw a movement away from the manufacture of goods at home (the 'Domestic System') to the manufacture of goods in factories.

Factory conditions

During the Industrial Revolution, factories and coalmines were dangerous places. They were organised to make a profit, with little concern for the safety of the workers. Children as young as four worked in the coalmines and some six-year-olds worked in factories. Working hours were very long and accidents were common, with children losing limbs and, in some cases, even their lives.

Reform and the reformers

The public were horrified when they heard about the conditions people – especially women and children – worked in. Some also wanted to improve the living conditions of the factory and mine workers.

Most politicians did not agree with social and political reform because of **laissez-faire** politics. However, some key individuals were **philanthropists** who continued to press for social and industrial reforms to improve the lives of the working class.

Reformer	Type of reform	Motivation	Actions
Michael Sadler MP	Factory	• Terrible conditions children worked in • Dangers of the machines • Poor treatment of children by the factory owner • Weight of coal being lifted by women and children	• Suggested maximum 10-hour day for those under 18 (the 10-hour movement)
Lord Shaftesbury	Factory and social	• Improving the lives of children both at work and socially • Christian faith	• Supporter of the Mines Act 1842 • Supported the 10-hour movement • Campaigned for more education for factory children
Robert Owen	Factory and social	• Mill owner but a socialist; thought a happy workforce was more important than profit	• Supported the 10-hour movement • Introduced an 8-hour day, 1810 • Opened a school at his New Lanark factory, 1816 • Social areas for workers to visit during time off
Edwin Chadwick	Social	• Improving living conditions for those in towns and cities • Improving the health of the population	• Wrote a report which linked sanitation with epidemics like cholera • Reported on the causes of poverty
Elizabeth Fry	Social	• Christian faith – Quaker • Helping the poor • Prison reform	• Opened a school and a chapel in Newgate Prison • Had prison reform raised in parliament • Conditions for women on transportation ships were improved
Josephine Butler	Social	• Family were involved in social reform and abolition • Christian faith – evangelical • Repealing the 1869 Contagious Disease Act	• Campaigned to protect women arrested for being prostitutes • Campaigned for the age of consent to rise from 13 to 16 • Contagious Disease Act repealed 1883

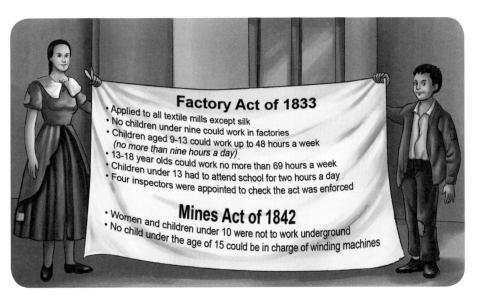

▲ Acts passed to reform working conditions

Impact of reforms

Many workers felt that the government's reform acts had not gone far enough. Poor people were still at a disadvantage and this was only made worse by the Poor Law Amendment Act of 1834. This sent people to the workhouse if they could not afford to care for their families.

They felt something had to change so they started to group together in trade unions.

SUMMARY

- New ideas in the nineteenth century started a period of reform.

- The Anti-Corn Law League put pressure on the government to repeal the Corn Laws so people could afford wheat.

- The abolition movement campaigned to abolish slavery in the British Empire.

- Workers in British factories were sometimes called 'white slaves', which inspired the abolition movement.

- New opinions on the working class inspired philanthropists to reform factories and living conditions.

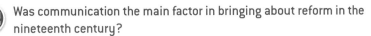 APPLY

FACTORS

a Write down all the methods used by the reformers. Then use different coloured highlighters to group the methods together for each of the following factors: communication, religion and politics.

b Read the exam question below and make a plan of what you will write in each paragraph of your answer, referring to the above factors.

c   Was communication the main factor in bringing about reform in the nineteenth century?

EXAMINER TIP

Think about all the different types of reform in the nineteenth century. There is a lot of information to consider, so making a quick plan is a good way to start an exam question.

REVIEW ↻

Look over Chapters 7 and 8 to help you answer this question.

EXAMINER TIP

For high-level answers you must make a judgement about the most important factor. Is there a factor that influences all reform groups in the nineteenth century?

REVISION SKILLS ✓

When making a judgement remember to support points with dates, key figures and key events. Practise for top marks by showing both opinions.

CHAPTER 9

Workers' movements

The start of trade unionism

In Medieval times workers joined Workers' Guilds that controlled wages and prices; businesses were small and conditions were good

→

During the Industrial Revolution wage competition was a big problem as there were so many workers; if someone complained about their wages they would be sacked and replaced

↓

The 1825 Combination Act allowed workers in the factories to come together in trade unions to negotiate wages and conditions but nothing else; they could not use intimidation or **picket**

←

New technology meant skilled workers were no longer needed; the Luddites and Swing Rioters opposed the new technology and damaged machines

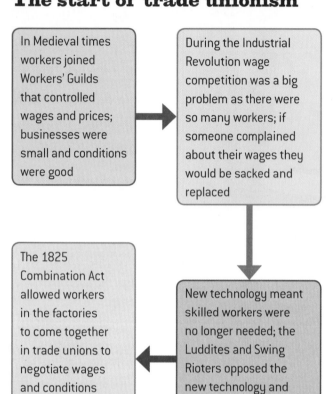

CASE STUDY:
THE TOLPUDDLE MARTYRS

WHO: SIX FARMERS LED BY GEORGE LOVELESS

WHERE: TOLPUDDLE, DORSET

WHEN: FEBRUARY 1834

WHY: FEWER FARM LABOURERS WERE NEEDED AND WAGES WERE DROPPING

WHAT: SWORE AN ILLEGAL OATH TO KEEP THEIR TRADE UNION A SECRET; ARRESTED AND TRANSPORTED TO AUSTRALIA TO ENDURE HARD LABOUR

REVISION SKILLS

Create timelines that show links between the different workers' groups. Many GNCTU members, after the Tolpuddle Martyrs, supported the Chartists.

REVIEW

Go back and look at Chapter 7 to help with this revision.

Grand National Consolidated Trades Union (GNCTU)

One of the earliest trade unions was the GNCTU, set up in 1833 by Robert Owen, who was important for factory and social reform (see Chapter 8). His aim was to bring all unions together under one organisation. Very soon the GNCTU had half a million members, but it struggled due to conflict between different groups of workers. The case of the Tolpuddle Martyrs shows the difficulties of early trade unions.

Word spread about the way the Tolpuddle Martyrs had been treated. Robert Owen called a meeting of the GNCTU and 10,000 attended.

Many supporters, including Robert Owen and William Cobbett, held a demonstration in Copenhagen Fields. Supporters gathered petitions and demanded the Tolpuddle Martyrs be returned to England. On 14 March 1836 the six men were given a full pardon; the trade unions had won.

New Model Unions

New Model Unions started in 1851 with the creation of the Amalgamated Society of Engineers (ASE). Others followed, with carpenters in 1860 and then tailors in 1866. They were seen as 'new model' because they:

• were highly skilled men
• could afford to pay subscriptions to ensure they received sick pay and other benefits
• did not want to destroy the structure they worked in
• negotiated rather than going on strike.

This 'new model' helped trade unions gain the support of the government. By the 1870s, trade unions had legal status and members could picket for their rights.

New Unionism

Although the New Model Unions had been successful, they had only benefited the more affluent skilled workers. The unskilled, working class were still very unhappy so took their own action. New Unionism was more militant than the New Model Unions; this can be seen clearly in two successful cases in the 1880s.

Both the match girls and the dockers were successful. Union membership increased and unskilled workers now had a voice.

CASE STUDY:
MATCHGIRLS' STRIKE

WHO: WOMEN AND GIRLS WHO MADE MATCHES

WHERE: BRYANT & MAY FACTORY, LONDON

WHEN: 1888

WHY: CONDITIONS IN THE FACTORY WERE POOR AND MANY OF THE WOMEN BECAME ILL, OFTEN FROM POISONING BY THE CHEMICALS IN THE MATCHES - THIS CAUSED 'PHOSSY JAW'; THEY WERE ALSO PAID POOR WAGES AND FREQUENTLY FINED

WHAT: WENT ON STRIKE WITH THE HELP OF A JOURNALIST, ANNIE BESANT, WHO PUBLISHED 'WHITE SLAVES OF LONDON' CALLING FOR A BOYCOTT OF MATCHES MADE AT BRYANT & MAY; MANY WORKERS SUPPORTED THE STRIKERS

CASE STUDY:
DOCKERS' STRIKE

WHO: DOCKERS. LED BY BEN TILLET

WHERE: LONDON

WHEN: 1889

WHY: WANTED A PAY INCREASE FROM FIVE PENCE TO SIX PENCE AN HOUR (DOCKER'S TANNER) AND MORE FOR OVERTIME; ALSO WANTED A GUARANTEED FOUR HOURS' WORK A DAY

WHAT: WENT ON STRIKE, MARCHED THROUGH LONDON CARRYING FISH HEADS AND ROTTEN VEGETABLES TO SHOW WHAT THEIR FAMILIES LIVED ON; ALSO PICKETED THE GATES OF THE LONDON DOCKS

▼  **SOURCE A** *A photograph of striking dockers in 1889; they are marching through London holding union banners*

SUMMARY

- The new unskilled working class of the Industrial Revolution wanted better pay and conditions.

- The government was worried about the threat of revolution, so took firm action against the unions at first.

- The skilled workers formed moderate unions and improved relationships with the government.

- The working class used New Unionism to fight for their rights and gain better terms and conditions.

 APPLY

SOURCE ANALYSIS

a Write a definition of trade unionism.

b Make revision cards and on each write the names of different trade unions and their different methods/actions. How much improvement in workers' rights did each achieve?

c EXAM QUESTION Study **Source A**. How useful is **Source A** to a historian researching the methods used by unions in the nineteenth century?

EXAMINER TIP

Although the source shows the Dockers' Strike you can still discuss other unions that marched as a form of protest.

Women's rights

RECAP

Different tactics

During the nineteenth century the rights of women in society had changed only slightly. Women were still legally very dependent on men, but many wanted more equality. To achieve this the law had to change and that meant women needed to be able to vote.

From 1897 to 1913 three main groups were created to campaign for the right for women to vote (known as female suffrage).

• National Union of Women's Suffrage Societies (NUWSS)

- Millicent Fawcett created the NUWSS in 1897– known as the Suffragists

- Believed in peaceful methods (meetings, speeches, letters, posters)

- Wanted to be seen as kind and gentle to persuade men to give them the vote

• The Women's Freedom League

- Created in 1907 by WSPU members who did not believe in violent tactics

- Mostly pacifists

- Also campaigned for equal pay for women

• All three

- Middle-class

- Wanted the vote for women

• Women's Social and Political Union (WSPU)

- Emmeline Pankhurst was a member of the Manchester NUWSS; she decided it was time for more direct action

- Formed WSPU in 1903 with her daughters Christabel and Sylvia – known as suffragettes

- Believed in 'deeds not words'

The NUWSS tried to get the vote by lobbying MPs, speaking publicly, creating petitions and distributing pamphlets. These did get some attention. However, the WSPU felt change was taking too long so they used more militant tactics:

- heckling MPs during speeches
- demonstrations outside the House of Commons
- chaining themselves to railings
- 1912 stone-throwing campaign: over 200 suffragettes arrested
- arson attacks and blowing up buildings.

REVISION SKILLS

Colour code the different groups when you are revising. This will help you remember and distinguish between the aims and methods of each group.

A suffragette martyr

Who: Emily Wilding Davison

When: 1913, Epsom Derby

What: Davison ran onto the track in front of the king's horse. She was trampled by the horse and died of her injuries.

Why: No one knows whether she meant to kill herself or simply to stick a suffragette rosette on the king's horse.

How is she remembered: Davison is regarded as the first martyr of the suffragette movement. It was now clear how far these women would go to get the vote.

Government response: The Cat and Mouse Act

Suffragettes were regularly arrested for their violent tactics. In prison they extended their protest by going on hunger strike. The government could not let the women die as they were from middle-class families with influential husbands or fathers. Also the government did not want to create martyrs. The women were initially force-fed but this was seen as too dangerous as it could lead to disabilities or death.

The government passed the Prisoners (Temporary Discharge for Ill Health) Act in 1913. The act said the women should be released when they became too weak due to starvation. Once they were well enough they would be rearrested and returned to prison. This became known as the 'Cat and Mouse Act'.

▼ **SOURCE A** *A poster produced by the National Women's Social and Political Union, c1910, of a suffragette hunger striker being force-fed in prison*

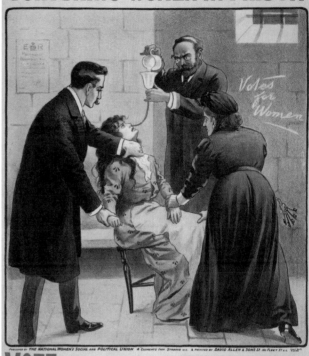

SOURCE ANALYSIS

a List everything you can find out from Source A about government responses to suffragette tactics.

b Explain the purpose of the poster.

c **EXAM QUESTION** Study **Source A**. How useful is **Source A** to a historian studying government reactions to suffragette tactics?

EXAMINER TIP

Include some contextual knowledge about how the suffragette movement changed around the date of the source. Why would the government be force-feeding the suffragettes? Use the image and the slogan.

Response to militancy

The suffragettes' aims and methods often met opposition. Many people thought:

- they held back women's suffrage because their violence made them look irrational and unbalanced — a good reason for not having the vote
- a woman's place was in the home
- politics was a man's world and women were unsuited to it; Prime Minister Herbert Asquith believed this and blocked moves to give women the vote.

War and the vote

The campaign for the vote was put on hold when the First World War broke out in 1914. The suffragettes joined the war effort, working in factories and doing other war work.

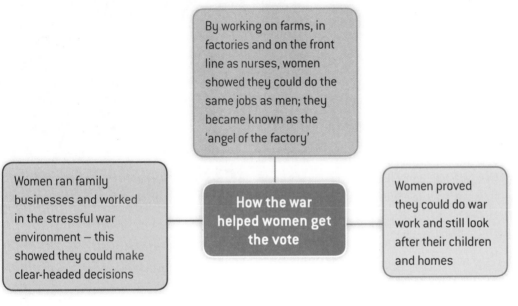

By working on farms, in factories and on the front line as nurses, women showed they could do the same jobs as men; they became known as the 'angel of the factory'

Women ran family businesses and worked in the stressful war environment — this showed they could make clear-headed decisions

How the war helped women get the vote

Women proved they could do war work and still look after their children and homes

Towards universal suffrage

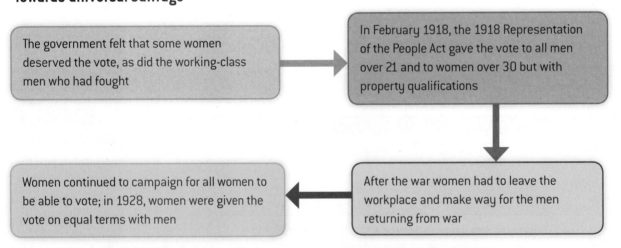

The government felt that some women deserved the vote, as did the working-class men who had fought

In February 1918, the 1918 Representation of the People Act gave the vote to all men over 21 and to women over 30 but with property qualifications

Women continued to campaign for all women to be able to vote; in 1928, women were given the vote on equal terms with men

After the war women had to leave the workplace and make way for the men returning from war

REVISION SKILLS

An important skill when revising is reducing lots of information into a clear, more concise form — this is sometimes known as 'chunking'. Try to reduce the information on women's suffrage into no more than an A5 sheet.

 154–159 | Revision progress

Equality in the later twentieth century

Women continued to campaign for greater equality, and in the 1960s the Women's Movement was born. This demanded:

- equal pay with men
- more women in higher education
- 24-hour child care
- free contraception and abortion on demand.

The movement wanted women to have the same rights and opportunities as men. It achieved some successes:

Timeline

▼ 1969
- Divorce Reform Act: allowed women to divorce their husbands and claim any property owned in the divorce settlement

▼ 1970
- Equal Pay Act: gave women the right to be paid the same as men for the same work

▼ 1975
- Sex Discrimination Act: Gave women rights and protection in the workplace

Today, women and men are not completely equal in society as there are still more men in higher education and there is still a wage gap. However, the suffragettes ensured that women could do something to change it: they could vote.

SUMMARY

- In the late nineteenth century a group of middle-class women started to fight for women to have the vote.

- Most people in society believed that politics was a man's world and no place for women.

- Emmeline Pankhurst started a new group, the WSPU, that would use more militant methods.

- During the First World War women stopped campaigning and worked to win the war.

- In 1918 some women gained voting rights and by 1929 women had the same voting rights as men.

- The fight for equality continued throughout the twentieth century.

 **APPLY**

EXPLAIN THE SIGNIFICANCE

a Describe women's involvement in politics before the First World War.

b Select five of the key events/dates that had an impact on women's rights and write a short summary of how each one changed women's lives.

c Select the one event that you think had the biggest impact. Explain your answer.

d
> **EXAM QUESTION** Explain the significance of the campaign for women's votes in the early twentieth century.

EXAMINER TIP

Think about how attitudes to women's rights and abilities have changed over time periods.

REVIEW

Read pages 48–49 on the tactics used by the suffragettes to help plan your answer to the significance question. You need to know what the suffragettes did if you are to explain the impact they had.

CHAPTER 11

Workers' rights

Causes of the General Strike, 1926

Impact of the First World War

During the war Britain's output had been high with lots of people working in industry. Coal  mines had been **nationalised**, but were returned to private owners afterwards. After 1918 there was a fall in demand for coal. Mine owners had to either close inefficient mines or introduce new automatic machinery that would mean fewer men were needed.

Technology

British coal mining struggled further because mines in countries like Germany and the USA had more modern equipment and lower costs. British mines could not compete so the unions called for the mines to be re-nationalised.

Mine owners and the unions

15 April 1921 (Black Friday): mine owners announced longer working hours but a drop in wages. The miners  decided to strike, but without the support of other big unions they had to go back to work or lose their jobs.

In 1925 the price of coal fell and the miners faced a further wage cut. Fearing a General Strike with the miners backed by other big unions, the government **subsidised** the coal industry.

Actions of the miners and government

In April 1926, when the government subsidy ran out, the miners did not want a pay cut. The TUC (Trades Union Congress) agreed to strike and on 3 May 1926 Britain's first General Strike began. It lasted for nine days with both sides using various tactics.

Government actions

- The army and university students took over essential jobs in industry
- Used own newspaper *The British Gazette* as propaganda to turn the public against the strike
- The army stopped the violent clashes between the strikers and government

TUC actions

- Strikers travelled to picket other industries and at times clashed violently with the police
- Used their newspaper *The British Worker* to explain reasons for the strike
- Set up funds to feed the families of strikers to help keep the strike going

Trade union reform

- The General Strike ended on 12 May 1926.
- The government won, as the unions ran out of money and the Labour Party did not support the strike.
- Miners had to return to work for lower wages and longer hours.
- The government passed the Trades Disputes and Trades Unions Act, 1927. It stopped unions joining together to strike or pay funds to a political party.

After the Second World War society changed and most key industries were nationalised. Trade union membership increased when the Labour government passed an amended Trades Disputes and Trade Unions Act. Increased union membership became a problem for the government when the 1960s brought an increase in prices and a drop in wages.

Timeline

▼ 1972 & 1974
- National Union of Miners vote for coal strikes which lead to three-day week

▼ 1974
- A new Labour government brings in a social contract that secures regular wage increases

▼ Winter 1978–79
- Series of strikes by public sector trade unions demanding larger pay rises (known as the Winter of Discontent)

▼ 1979
- Conservatives come to power under Margaret Thatcher; begin to challenge power of unions

▼ 1980 & 1982
- Employment Acts introduced, making it unlawful for someone to be fired because they are not in a union; it also gives employers more power to fire striking employees

▼ 1984
- Miners' Strike; government introduces Trade Union Act, making it harder to strike legally

▼ 1985
- Miners' Strike ends; government has control over trade unions

Key to timeline:

- Conservative government – Prime Minister: Heath 1970–74
- Labour government – Prime Minister: Wilson then Callaghan 1974–79
- Conservative government – Prime Minister: Thatcher 1979–90

SUMMARY

- After the First World War prices for industrial goods fell.
- Miners and other groups called for nationalisation to save their jobs.
- There was an increase in union activity, resulting in the General Strike.
- The government passed laws to restrict union activity.
- After the Second World War union power grew and strikes could paralyse essential services.
- The government took action to limit the powers of the unions in the late twentieth century.

⚙ APPLY

FACTORS

a. Make a list of the different tactics used by trade unions in the twentieth century.

b. Make flashcards of the key government responses to trade union activity throughout the twentieth century.

c. What do you think was the main factor in the development of trade unionism in the twentieth century? Explain your answer.

EXAMINER TIP

This activity will help you plan an answer or a practice question about trade unionism. Factors you may consider are communication, economy and politics.

REVISION SKILLS

Remember to include key dates, the names of prime ministers and their party, along with the impact of the response. Without this information your cards won't be so useful for revision.

REVIEW

You may wish to look back at Chapter 9 about trade unionism in the nineteenth century.

CHAPTER 12

Minority rights

Immigration in the twentieth century

After the First and Second World Wars, Britain's large empire began to shrink as many countries became independent from that empire. Some countries kept ties with Britain though, by becoming part of the Commonwealth.

The British government needed to rebuild the country after the war and there was a shortage of people to work in low paid and unskilled jobs. The government invited people from Commonwealth countries to come to live and work in Britain.

- The 1948 British Nationality Act gave all Commonwealth citizens the chance to move to Britain.
- If they came to the 'Mother Country' they could gain full British citizenship.
- People from Commonwealth countries were keen to see what Britain was like and to benefit from new opportunities.
- The British Government gave interest-free loans so that immigrants could afford the cost of travelling by ship.
- Recruitment fairs in countries like Jamaica helped immigrants secure a job before they had left their home country.

On 22 June 1948 the ship *Empire Windrush* docked near London with 492 people from the Caribbean on board. Over the next decade more immigrants arrived from the Caribbean and Asia.

The immigrant experience

Social	• The first wave of immigrants were mostly young black men; they clashed with groups of young white men • In the areas that immigrants had moved to there was **segregation**
Employment	• Many immigrants were forced to do low paid, unskilled work as their qualifications were not recognised • Doctors arrived from the Indian **subcontinent** and worked in the new National Health Service • Many Asian immigrants started their own businesses in their communities
Housing	• Many white people moved out of areas that immigrants moved to – this was known as 'white flight' • Many landlords and even housing associations tried to stop black and Asian people renting their houses

Tensions came to a head in 1958 with the Notting Hill Riots. Many people felt there were too many immigrants in the major cities and relations between the immigrants and some white residents grew worse. Black people found it harder to get work, as factory owners and other employers refused to employ immigrants. Something had to change.

Government reform

Timeline

▶ 1962	▶ 1968	▶ 1971
■ Commonwealth Immigrants Act: Immigrants need to apply for a work voucher to come to Britain; they can only get one if their skills are in demand	■ Commonwealth Immigrants Act: Even those from the Commonwealth who hold a British passport cannot come to Britain unless they have a parent or grandparent who was born in or a citizen of the UK; possibly introduced out of fear that 200,000 Asians living in Kenya might come to Britain to escape discrimination, due to policy of Africanisation being introduced in Kenya	■ Immigration Act: Immigrants can only get temporary work permits; also encourages voluntary repatriation – the government will help people move back to their country of origin and change their citizenship back

The government sent a clear message with these reforms. They wanted to reduce the number of immigrants, but the reforms were viewed as an attempt to simply reduce non-white immigration.

REVISION SKILLS

Remembering dates is important but make sure you link an event to its outcome. This is how you explain impact.

APPLY

SOURCE ANALYSIS

▶ **SOURCE A** *A cartoon created by Victor Weisz for the* Evening Standard, *1961; the caption reads, 'The Commonwealth can be an example to other nations' and is a quote from Prime Minister Harold Macmillan to the Commonwealth Parliamentary Conference, where the government discussed the Commonwealth Immigrants Act*

a Describe Source A. What can you see happening?

b What message is the cartoonist of Source A trying to convey?

c Why was this cartoon drawn in 1961?

d Write a paragraph describing the links between the features of Source A to government acts about immigration.

e **EXAM QUESTION** Study **Source A**. How useful is **Source A** to a historian studying government responses to immigration in the twentieth century?

"The Commonwealth can be an example to other nations."
—MR. MACMILLAN, ADDRESSING THE COMMONWEALTH PARLIAMENTARY CONFERENCE ON SEPTEMBER

EXAMINER TIP

Remember to connect what you see in the source to events that happened before, during and after the time the source was produced. You may want to consider the role of the Race Relations Act when deciding how useful the source is. See page 56 for details of the act.

Enoch Powell

The feeling that government acts were racist was fuelled by the politics of Enoch Powell. He was a Conservative MP who was very outspoken about immigration. He gave a famous speech in 1968 which became known as the 'Rivers of Blood' speech.

Powell's politics had the following impact:

- He gained a lot of support, especially from the working class.
- Supporters of 'Powellism' believed that white people were superior to non-white people, even those born in Britain.
- Powellism encouraged the politics of the National Front, a group who wanted all non-white people to return to their family's country of origin.

We must be mad, literally mad, as a nation to be permitting the annual inflow of some 50,000 dependants … So insane are we that we actually permit unmarried persons to immigrate …

Race Relations Act

With the rise of Powellism and official policy against immigration, the black and Asian community in Britain were feeling disillusioned. They needed to be reassured that the government represented them as well.

Government Acts

- 1965 Race Relations Act: prevented racial discrimination in housing and employment; no criminal convictions were ever brought before the Race Relations Board
- 1968 Commonwealth Immigrants Act: aimed to help the integration of immigrant communities
- 1976 Race Relations Act: stated that discrimination meant any practice that put another group at a disadvantage; replaced Race Relations Board with more powerful Commission for Racial Equality

Brixton Riots, 1981

The 1976 Race Relations Act was seen as a failure, as within five years there were riots in Brixton and in major cities around the UK. On the surface the riots were about poor relations between the black community and the police. However, there were many other reasons for the riots:

Economic: In Britain in the late 1970s there was a recession and this economic hardship hit black communities the hardest with high unemployment, poor housing and higher crime rates.

Political: In 1977 the Battle of Lewisham was caused by a National Front march through the borough of Lewisham, which was predominantly a black area. The National Front was convinced that black people were more likely to be involved in crime and this made them even more against multi-cultural societies.

Social: A new law allowed the police to stop and search anyone they suspected was about to commit a crime – known as the 'sus law'. Many people saw this as racial profiling and felt that more black people were being stopped because of their skin colour.

All of these factors meant when 1000 people were stopped in six days in Brixton under 'sus law', tension increased as young black men felt attacked in their own community.

Rumours of police brutality and the arrest of a young black man on 10 April 1981 sparked the start of the Brixton Riots. For three days the black community fought the police, and set fire to cars and buildings.

After Brixton, Lord Scarman was asked to write a report on events.

An investigation in the 1990s proved that the Metropolitan Police Service did suffer from institutional racism after their poor response to the murder of Stephen Lawrence – a racially motivated attack – in 1993.

SCARMAN REPORT

- NO INSTITUTIONAL RACISM IN THE METROPOLITAN POLICE SERVICE

- SUGGESTED MAKING RACIALLY PREJUDICED BEHAVIOUR AN OFFENCE

- ENDED THE 'SUS LAW'

- LED TO THE CREATION OF THE POLICE COMPLAINTS AUTHORITY

SUMMARY

- After the Second World War the British government needed workers to fill jobs in new industries.
- People from Commonwealth countries were encouraged to come to Britain and gain citizenship.
- The government had to introduce new policies on immigration as tension grew between communities.
- The Brixton Riots brought tension between police and the black community to a head.
- Government and police reforms were introduced after the Scarman Report.

REVISION SKILLS

Repetition is vital for good long-term memory. Plan revision sessions in short bursts of 20 to 30 minutes several times a day.

APPLY

SIMILARITY

a Make a mind-map to show the reasons for tension between white and non-white communities. Use the headings: political, social and economic.

b Describe the outcome of the Brixton Riots. Think about short- and long-term impacts.

c EXAM QUESTION Explain two ways in which the people who rioted in Brixton and the suffragettes were similar.

EXAMINER TIP

You should consider the methods both groups used and their outcomes. Government policies are a key similarity.

REVIEW

Look again at pages 48–51 about the suffragettes.

GCSE sample answers

 REVIEW

On these exam practice pages, you will find a sample student answer for each of the exam questions for Paper 2 Britain: Power and the People Thematic Study. What are the strengths and weaknesses of the answers? Read the following pages and think carefully about what the student has written, what the examiner has said about each answer, and how you might improve your own answers to the Power and the People exam questions.

The source analysis question

◀ **SOURCE A** *An American poster published on 28 March 1770 showing 'the Boston Massacre' of 5 March 1770, when British soldiers fired on a crowd of civilians. The massacre took place in front of the Royal Custom House, which is labelled 'Butcher's Hall' in the poster. The title of the picture was 'The Fruits of Arbitrary Power', or 'The Bloody Massacre' and it was reprinted many times*

 EXAM QUESTION 1 Study **Source A**. How useful is **Source A** to a historian studying the American Revolution? Explain your answer by using **Source A** and your contextual knowledge.

8 marks

Sample student answer

Source A is useful to a historian studying why the American Revolution started as it shows how the British used force when dealing with their colony – it shows the British firing on the colonists after being directed by their officer in the background. The title of the picture mentions 'arbitrary power' which is one of the main objections the Americans had to British rule. The British imposed taxes on the colonists and refused them representation in parliament. The colonists did begin to fight back but the British used force to suppress them as they were scared they would lose their most important part of the empire. They made money from trading American goods such as sugar, and used America as a penal colony. A historian studying the causes of the American Revolution would find this source useful as it shows the changing relationship between Britain and the colonists.

 EXAMINER TIP

Try not to write only about what you can see in the picture but also about what facts you know. For example, the tax the British made the colonists pay was a key cause of the American Revolution.

 EXAMINER TIP

The question asks about 'how useful' the source is, and this answer directly refers to the changing relationship between Britain and its colony. The answer shows that the British started to use force and goes some way to explain why this was the case.

OVERALL COMMENT

The answer is a good answer at Level 3 because it uses what can be seen in the picture and adds some extra knowledge. It also uses the provenance of the source in the answer. To secure a Level 4 the points from the provenance would need to be more developed.

OVER TO YOU

1 Review the sample answer:

   a highlight where the answer adds some factual knowledge

   b highlight where the answer uses the provenance (caption information).

2 **a** Now have a go at writing your own answer. Remember, in the exam it is recommended that you spend no more than 10 minutes on this question.

   b Once you have written your answer, check it against the questions below. Did you…

    ☐ include some detailed facts and figures?

    ☐ remember to refer to the provenance of the source?

    ☐ make your answer relevant to what the historian is studying?

You may find it helpful to look back at Chapter 6 to refresh your knowledge of the American Revolution.

The 'significance' question

 EXAM QUESTION

2 Explain the significance of the Chartists.

8 marks

Sample student answer

The Chartists are significant because they forced the government to think about the rights of the working class and to reform the electoral system. The movement made sure the issue of electoral reform was one the government could not ignore; they did this by sending three petitions to parliament. This was especially important after the Great Reform Act of 1832 had given some men the vote; however, this was mostly the middle class. More change was needed. Another way the Chartists tried to secure this change was by publishing their own newspaper. This allowed the movement to organise workers and gain more support – more people could find out about the Chartists which helped them to have a bigger impact.

   The Chartists are also significant because they influenced other movements. The suffragette movement which was campaigning for female suffrage was influenced by the Chartists and even had both a militant and peaceful wing, as the Chartists had done. However, the significance of the Chartists was reduced in the early twentieth century – it had been a movement focused on the vote

EXAMINER TIP

Activities **1a** and **b** will help you build your own answer. Remember to always start by describing what you can see in the source, then identify what this tells you about the question being asked, and then finally add in your own knowledge.

EXAMINER TIP

There were many causes of the American Revolution. You could mention the border disputes in the West and the different taxes that were imposed by the British. Overall, Source A shows a changing relationship between Britain and America, so explain why that happened.

EXAMINER TIP

The answer shows a range of accurate knowledge and understanding that is relevant to the question.

for all men, not women, so it was criticised when the focus turned to female suffrage. Furthermore, the Chartists are significant because many men involved in the Chartist movement went on to join the trade union movement which changed workers' rights at the time.

EXAMINER TIP

The answer explains two aspects of significance. Firstly, how the Chartists changed things in the short term and secondly, their influence on other campaigning groups.

EXAMINER TIP

Provide some detail to show how this idea of workers' rights developed over time. To help with this read Chapter 11.

OVERALL COMMENT

This answer is largely a Level 3 response but does show some elements of a Level 4. It gives two developed points of significance and attempts to show how the significance of the movement changed over time.

OVER TO YOU

1   Review the sample answer:

   a   highlight the technical terms used in the answer

   b   highlight where the answer mentions the Chartists' impact.

2   **a**   Now have a go at writing your own answer. Remember, in the exam it is recommended that you spend no more than 10 minutes on this question.

   b   Once you have written your answer, check it against the questions below. Did you…

   ☐   include some detailed knowledge?

   ☐   remember to provide at least two examples of the significance of the Chartists?

You may find it helpful to look back at Chapter 7 to refresh your knowledge of the Chartists.

EXAMINER TIP

You should explain how the Chartists' Temperance Movement and links with the Cooperative Movement make the Chartists significant. Try to show how these ideas link with other movements.

The 'similarity/difference' question

> **EXAM QUESTION**   3   Explain two ways in which Simon de Montfort and the Pankhursts were similar.
>
> **8 marks**

Sample student answer

Simon de Montfort and the Pankhursts both challenged authority and made society fairer. Simon de Montfort forced Henry III to sign the Provisions of Oxford in 1258 which increased the power the barons had. The Pankhursts formed the WSPU in 1903 to increase the power women had by giving them the vote. They were successful, as in 1918 women over the age of 30 got the vote and then in

EXAMINER TIP

This answer is good because it immediately identifies a similarity.

1928 women finally gained the vote on equal terms with men. Simon de Montfort and the Pankhursts are similar in terms of long term impact as de Montfort invited the commoners to parliament for the first time – groups like the burgesses then featured in Edward I's Model Parliament in 1295 and still do today. Likewise, the suffragettes influenced the Women's Movement in Britain. They campaigned for further equality for women with four clear demands: 24-hour child care, more women in higher education, equal pay, and free contraception and abortion on demand. The 100-year anniversary celebrations of the Representation of the People Act 1918 also show the significance of the suffragettes in the long term.

EXAMINER TIP

This answer could have reached Level 4 if it had provided some detail about how the two time periods were similar – both were times when the king/government did not want to change the law.

EXAMINER TIP

The student has given developed reasoning for two identified similarities.

OVERALL COMMENT

This answer is a high Level 3. It shows some detailed knowledge but might be improved by adding more detail or explanation about the similarities of the different time periods, for example that those in power were reluctant to change and often went back on their word, so both groups faced opposition.

OVER TO YOU

1   Review the sample answer:

   a   highlight where the answer shows it is concerned with similarity

   b   highlight where the answer shows relevant knowledge

   c   highlight where the answer adds knowledge that is not directly related to the question.

2 **a**   Now have a go at writing your own answer. Remember, in the exam it is recommended that you spend no more than 10 minutes on this question.

   b   Once you have written your answer, check it against the questions below. Did you…

   ☐   suggest two similarities?

   ☐   make sure that they share a common theme or point?

   ☐   include some detailed facts from your own knowledge to support each similarity?

You may find it helpful to look back at Chapters 2 and 10 to refresh your knowledge of the Middle Ages and the early twentieth century.

EXAMINER TIP

You could use your understanding of factors to plan this question by thinking about what factors both people/ groups have in common.

The 'main factors' question

  4   Have economic factors been the main cause of protest in Britain? Explain your answer with reference to economic and other factors.

|16 marks|

|SPaG 4 marks|

Sample student answer

The economy has been an important factor in causing protest in Britain from Medieval times to the present day. The Peasants' Revolt was caused by the poll tax that Edward III had imposed on all citizens over the age of 15, along with the Statute of Labourers which stopped peasants being able to compete for higher wages. In the nineteenth century most protest was caused by the economy, as can be seen with the Anti-Corn Law League which was committed to ending the Corn Laws that were introduced in 1815. The Corn Laws stopped workers being able to afford bread; they were laws that benefited the land owners and politicians. The Luddites and Swing Rioters, although enraged by new technology, were ultimately driven by the loss of the money they had made as skilled tradesmen when their livelihoods were ruined by the new machines of the Industrial Revolution. Similarly, the twentieth century saw further protest fuelled by the economy during the miners' strike of 1984.

Although the economy has been important, the most important factor in causing protest has been government actions. From the Medieval period to the present day it has been policies imposed on people or the king/government's reluctance to change society that has caused the most protests. The Pilgrimage of Grace was a protest against the religious reforms imposed by Henry VIII and Thomas Cromwell with the dissolution of the monasteries. In the nineteenth century the gathering on Copenhagen Fields to protest the transportation of the Tolpuddle Martyrs was also about the limitations put on trade unions by the government. In the twentieth century the Brixton Riots are a good example of what can happen when the government continues to impose laws and restrictions on one community.

EXAMINER TIP

This answer is good because it uses examples of protest from many different time periods.

EXAMINER TIP

This point should be developed to explain why government responses are more important than economy and another factor. Try to show how the three factors influence each other.

EXAMINER TIP

The answer will gain marks because it has plenty of factual knowledge to support its understanding.

OVERALL COMMENT

The answer is good because it uses examples of economy from across the whole time period covered by the unit, 'Power and the People'. It is a strong Level 3 because it has explained how economy as well as government actions have caused protest. There is good spelling and grammar in the answer and it uses the correct historical terms. However, to be sure of a Level 3 mark it would benefit from another factor. For Level 4 the judgement about government actions being the most important factor should be developed and then compared to another factor to show 'relative impact'.

OVER TO YOU

1 Review the sample answer. Highlight where the following are mentioned:

   a specific protests

   b government actions

   c how each factor acted to cause protest.

2 Now have a go at writing your own answer. Remember, in the exam it is recommended that you spend no more than 20 minutes on this question.

   a Write a paragraph about another factor involved in protests, such as new ideas, social issues and religion.

   b Write a conclusion in which you compare the influence of the main factor with another factor.

   c Once you have written your answer, check it against the questions below. Did you...

   ☐ write about a factor other than the one mentioned in the question?

   ☐ add some factual knowledge of your own?

   ☐ make a decision about which factor was the main factor?

   ☐ check your answer for correct spellings, punctuation and grammar?

EXAMINER TIP

You only have 20 minutes to answer this question so a paragraph should take about 5 minutes.

EXAMINER TIP

When planning your response to this question try to show how factors link together. This will help you explain 'relative impact' in your response.

Activity answers guidance

The answers provided here are examples, based on the information provided in the Recap sections of this Revision Guide. There may be other factors which are relevant to each question, and you should draw on as much of your own knowledge as possible to give detailed and precise answers. There are also many ways of answering exam questions (for example, of structuring an essay). However, these exemplar answers should provide a good starting point.

Chapter 1
Page 13
SOURCE ANALYSIS

a Qualities might include:
   i   defend the people by leading the army well
   ii keep the country peaceful
   iii successfully deal with any rebellions
   iv maintain good relations with the Church.

   Why they were important:
   i   countries at this time were in constant threat of invasion
   ii the king should listen to his people and maintain good relations – wars meant taxes had to be raised and that angered people
   iii the king should look strong and have control over his subjects
   iv the Church was the centre of life for all Medieval people and there was a real fear of going to hell.

b **Successes:** Religious tolerance and a fair justice system

   Failures: Poor war record with lots of land being lost to the French; excommunicated by the Pope; unhappy barons due to increased taxes

c You might include that the source shows King John engaged in battle. We know from the provenance that he lost the Battle of Bouvines and this makes it useful to a historian studying the barons' dissatisfaction with John's rule, as Medieval kings were expected to lead their army well but King John lost this and many other battles. It is useful evidence for why the barons gave him the nicknames 'lackland' and 'softsword'. Furthermore, we know from the provenance that John had to pay a lot of money to bring the war to an end. This also makes the source useful as another reason the barons were dissatisfied with the king was because he had to raise taxes to fund his wars with France. The provenance makes the source useful as it is a picture from a history of France showing that the French victory over John was important.

FACTORS

Page 15

- **Role of the individual:** You could also talk about the Pope and his support for John's opposition to Magna Carta. This caused more disagreements with the barons and led to the Siege of Rochester and the First Barons' War.
- **Government:** You could write about the barons' desire for more power and that

eventually Magna Carta introduced the idea that there were some laws and rules the king had to follow.
- **Economy:** The barons were angry that they had to pay scutage and other taxes to fund John's wars in France. This especially angered the barons as John lost most wars he fought.
- **Religion:** John's excommunication by the Pope led to disagreements as the Church was at the centre of Medieval life. John was failing as a king and this made the barons angry.

Chapter 2
Page 17
FACTORS

a Your table might include:

   Problem with Henry's rule / Factor / How important:

   - He was pious and this meant he was willing to support the Pope financially in many of his war campaigns / Religion / Big problem as Henry was more concerned about upsetting the Pope than upsetting the barons
   - Had to win his father, King John's, land back in France/ Government / Medium problem as he would need to raise taxes to fight the wars, but if he was successful this would be good for England
   - Henry gave jobs to friends and foreign nationals / Government / Big problem as the barons didn't want to feel that they were losing their power and influence
   - The Pope wanted money for wars / Economic / Big problem as this meant raising more money in taxes but Henry did not want to anger the Pope
   - The Pope threatened to excommunicate Henry / Religion / Big problem as King John's excommunication had been one of the main causes of the barons making him sign Magna Carta

   The rating 1–5 is your opinion.

b You should create your own mind-map for this activity.

SIMILARITY

Your answer might include:
- both challenged royal authority by giving more power to the Great Council/ parliament
- both were movements run by the barons and their outcomes were to benefit that group only and not those at the bottom of the feudal system

- both were unsuccessful in the short term but had successful long term impacts
- the economy was a cause of both.

Page 19
SIGNIFICANCE

a He called the burgesses and knights to the Great Council.

   He reconfirmed Magna Carta and the Provisions of Oxford.

b The biggest change was that in the 1295 parliament the commoners were elected, and Edward called lots of parliaments which meant decisions were made in a more democratic way.

c We still have a parliament that resembles the 1295 parliament (which was inspired by de Montfort).
   - The king's power continued to be challenged throughout the Medieval period.
   - As Simon de Montfort had ruled without a king this gave inspiration to the English Civil War.
   - Our current monarch is a constitutional monarch and has no direct influence over the government.

d The 1265 parliament is significant as it was the first time that 'commoners' had been invited to the Great Council to be heard. Simon de Montfort invited the burgesses from the towns and cities as he needed support against Henry and those barons who were concerned about his increasing power. By inviting the burgesses, Simon de Montfort changed the way democracy worked in the Middle Ages. This was clear when Edward I called his Model Parliament in 1295. He had learned from his father's mistakes and knew he would need to listen to the Great Council if he wanted to remain on the throne.

   The 1265 parliament has had an impact on today as our parliament resembles the 1295 one with elected commons. Furthermore, the challenges to royal authority after the 1265 parliament have developed over time as now we have a constitutional monarch who has no direct influence over parliament. The 1265 parliament paved the way for Britain to be a democracy.

Chapter 3
Page 21
FACTORS

a and b

This is personal choice, but when you are considering the main causes of the

Peasants' Revolt the economy and religion are key factors. The poll tax that had been introduced was arguably the trigger for making the peasants revolt. This links with religion as the church was making people pay pardons for their sins, money that the peasants did not have. Social and political factors were important but were not the main causes because they feed in to the economy. The introduction of the Statute of Labourers was important and the Black Death was a key reason the peasants felt more powerful. However, the Statute of Labourers and the Black Death highlighted how unfairly they were being treated and how poor their wages were. Remember though, there is no right or wrong answer so long as you can support your argument with good examples and explanations.

Page 23
SIMILARITY

a **Short-term:** poll tax stopped, end of the Statute of Labourers, peasants continued to earn more money

   Long term: peasants were freemen, poll tax did not return until 1989

b The signing of Magna Carta and the Peasants' Revolt are similar as they were both caused by economic factors. The signing of Magna Carta was due, in part, to the barons' dissatisfaction with King John and the taxes he charged, such as scutage, to fight wars in France. The Peasants' Revolt was also motivated by tax as Richard II charged a poll tax of 4 groats to everyone over the age of 15. This tax was also used to fund wars in France. Another similarity is the outcome of both events. In both cases the king went back on his word. When King John signed Magna Carta at Runnymede in 1215 he promised to rule according to Magna Carta, however, with support from the Pope he quickly went back on his word, bringing about the First Barons' War. Richard II made a similar move while meeting with Wat Tyler and the peasants on 15 June. He agreed to their demands but then one of his men killed Wat Tyler and Richard sent the peasants home with no intention of meeting their demands.

Chapter 4
Page 25
FACTORS

a Martin Luther was frustrated that the Catholic Church was making people pay indulgences for their sins. He also believed everyone should be able to read the Bible, not just those who read Latin.

b Your answer might include:
   - He created the Church of England, and made himself head of it, to help him get a divorce and to reduce the power of the Pope.

- He put Cromwell in charge of collecting money from the monasteries.
- He closed as many monasteries as he could, using the excuse that they weren't spending money wisely.

c Your timeline should include the following dates and events: 1517 – Martin Luther publishes his writings, 1534 – Henry's Act of Supremacy makes him head of the Church of England, 1536 – rebellion in Yorkshire begins the Pilgrimage of Grace.

d **Role of the individual:** Cromwell being the king's adviser; Henry's self-interest.

   Religion: Henry breaking from Rome and creating the Church of England; closing the monasteries.

   Economy: Removing the Pope as the head of the Church so he did not have to pay tax to the Pope; Henry acquiring more wealth by removing it from the monasteries.

   Government: Advisers who were supporters of Catherine being removed from court; Cromwell being the key adviser.

Page 27
SIGNIFICANCE

a The Pilgrimage of Grace made an impact in the short term as the 'rebels' secured support in the north of England against the king's policies. In the long term the Pilgrimage of Grace secured Henry's power as there were no other rebellions during his reign; he had shown that he was too powerful to challenge.

b This is your opinion but you should support your point with all the relevant content you can. If you want to secure a Level 4 you should always get in the habit of comparing points to show how they influence one another.

c The Pilgrimage of Grace is significant because in the short term it helped Henry secure more power. Politically, Henry VIII became more powerful after the Pilgrimage of Grace and saw no more rebellions. He also strengthened his control of the north of England. In the long term it allowed Henry to secure the wealth he had craved. Henry secured funding to improve his navy and helped defend England. The Pilgrimage of Grace also led to the dissolution of larger monasteries which Henry could authorise with little opposition.

SOURCE ANALYSIS

The source is useful because:

- it shows Henry using the Pope as a footstool, which demonstrates the disregard Henry had for the Pope. This positioning is to make it seem that Henry is against the Pope. This move away from the Pope in Rome was a key cause of the Pilgrimage of Grace.

- Henry is sitting on a very high throne making him look powerful. This was the case after the Pilgrimage of Grace, because a key consequence of the uprising was that Henry became more powerful; he saw no more rebellions during his reign.
- we can tell that Henry had lots of money from his clothes and weapons. His wealth increased after the Pilgrimage of Grace, and this had been his main motivation for the dissolution of the monasteries.

Chapter 5
Page 29
FACTORS

You should make your own choices about the factors involved in each event. You will find that some of the events come under more than one factor.

SOURCE ANALYSIS

a Charles allowed William Laud to change the way people worshipped. He introduced a new prayer book to Scotland. His changes to religion made people worry that he might be a Catholic.

b Scottish Presbyterians were so upset as the new reforms to religion relied on the catechism and this was in direct conflict with the way Protestants worshipped.

c They might be presenting the prayer book to Charles to show him how closely linked it is to Catholicism, or confronting him with it as the cause of their discontent. They might also be trying to get him to take it back!

d You could say the following:
   - He looks ready for war.
   - His body language suggests resistance.
   - He is made to look better than the Covenanters.
   - He has been made to look quite 'fancy' – this is the opposite of how the Presbyterians would dress.

e Your answer might state that the source is useful as it shows that Charles' relationship with the Scots was a main cause of the English Revolution as the Scots were upset by the new Laudian reforms, especially the new prayer book which one of the Covenanters is holding. Scotland was Presbyterian and so the new prayer book that relied on catechism upset the congregations such as those in St Giles in 1637 when the book was first introduced. The source also shows Charles ready for war and it was his request for money from parliament to fight the Scots that sparked the war, especially during 1640 with the Long and Short Parliaments.

On the other hand the source is clearly Scottish or parliament propaganda as it shows the Covenanters showing respect to the king by removing their hats. The artist wanted us to see the Covenanters as fair and probably the just side, so it is useful as a piece of propaganda and to show how the Covenanters viewed Charles and his changes to religion.

Page 31
FACTORS

a Your spider diagram should include the start of the Civil War, key battles/events and new ideas. Think about the role of the New Model Army, Oliver Cromwell and King Charles. You should also include the impacts of the Civil War, such as political radicalism.

b Oliver Cromwell's aims were:
   • royal reforms
   • to remove the king
   • to create more parliamentary authority
   • to have an army that was built on ability rather than position in society.

c The New Model Army was new because for the first time soldiers could be promoted without privilege but rather because of their ability. The army was disciplined and had to live by a strict religious code; they could not drink or swear. The New Model Army also used new tactics. For example at the Battle of Naseby they approached slowly rather than charging and they attacked from the rear. The royalist army was not prepared for this new approach.

Page 33
SIGNIFICANCE

a • Taxation
   • His favourites
   • Religious reforms
   • His wife was Catholic
   • He would not listen to parliament

b There were various reasons:

   moral: Some, including Cromwell, felt that the king would need to die to allow society to become fairer; they felt the king had betrayed the bond of trust with his subjects.

   religious: There was the feeling that the defeat of Charles was God's desire and so was his execution.

   political: New ideas meant ordinary people felt they should be listened to and that they should have influence.

   economic: People wanted political control of taxation.

c **Economy**

   Charles I: Charged taxes and dissolved parliament when it would not support his demands for funds

   After Civil War: Cromwell improved the economy with Navigations Acts and the economy was controlled by parliament

   Religion

   Charles: No religious tolerance and reforms imposed on all, even the Presbyterian Scots

After Civil War: Jews returned to England and there was freedom to worship

Politics

Charles: Believed in the divine right of kings and did not listen to parliament

After Civil War: New, radical ideas emerged, such as those held by the Levellers and Diggers, that were based on a more equal society; England's reputation as a great power was restored

d The English Revolution is significant as it completely challenged the authority of the monarchy. This had been attempted several times but unsuccessfully with the signing of Magna Carta and the Provisions of Oxford. After the English Revolution we had a republic and parliament in control of the country. This was secured even after the restoration of the monarchy in 1660.

Chapter 6
Page 35
FACTORS

a and b Your flashcards could include the following points:

   Short-term:

   Politics: Boundary disputes with Native Americans; British force used at Lexington; declaration of independence

   Economy: Boston Tea Party

   Long-term:

   Politics: No representation in Britain

   Economy: pay for the British Army to be in North America; the Navigation Acts which restricted trade; taxes on things such as tea

c The political situation in America when it was ruled by Britain was the main cause of the American revolution. America was part of Britain's empire and Britain ruled the colony using force. This is one of the ways that politics is a short-term cause as the British killed anti-British colonists in Boston in 1770; this event would be remembered as the Boston Massacre. This increased anti-British feeling in America. The key political issue for the colonists in America was the fact that the British would impose taxes and border limits on them and they had no say in parliament. This led to their slogan: 'No taxation without representation!' Finally, a Declaration of Independence made it clear that America wanted to be politically free from Britain, but they would need to fight for this freedom.

Chapter 7
Page 37
SIMILARITY

a Petitions; speeches; gatherings/ demonstrations; formed political unions; put pressure on government

b You could make profiles for: Henry Hunt, Thomas Attwood, the BPU, and Earl Grey.

c Your answer might include the following:

   It was 'great' because it helped the middle class gain more representation and gave representation to new towns and cities. It proved that change was possible.

   It was not 'great' because many working-class people did not earn enough to qualify for the vote and there was still no secret ballot.

d The American colonists and early nineteenth century parliamentary reformers are similar in regard to their methods. Both movements petitioned government for more representation and when that was denied they resorted to more extreme methods. The Boston Tea Party and the BPU's call for the working class to stop paying tax are similar as they were events that challenged the authority of the British government to claim tax, but they were also the grand gestures that made the government take notice of each group's aims. Both campaigns had violent episodes with the Boston Massacre in 1770 and Peterloo in 1819; both events see some of those seeking reform being killed by the British authorities.

Page 39
SOURCE ANALYSIS

a Your mind-map could have the following points for the two arms:

   Lovett: petitions, pamphlets, temperance newspapers

   O'Connor: violence (plug plot), newspapers, called for a general strike

b You could include the following points: Rejected petitions, put up posters, asked people not to attend Chartist meetings, arrested the Chartist leaders, ordered transportation, killed protestors (Newport Rising)

c Your timeline should include the following dates and events: 1832 (Great Reform Act), 1834 (Poor Law), 1836 (Chartist movement started), 1839 (first petition), 1842 (second petition), 1847 (economic and agricultural depression), 1848 (third petition).

d Source A shows a Chartist at the beginning of a protest who is shouting. It then shows the same person next to a policeman who has stopped the protest by showing his baton. In the first part of the picture it looks as though the crowd is going mad.

e The source is useful to a historian studying the failure of Chartism as it shows a crowd of people demonstrating and being rowdy and then a policeman threatening to use his baton. This shows that the Chartists had become violent in their methods and that the police had to use force. This is useful as the source was created in 1849 after the third petition had been sent to parliament by Feargus O'Connor. A crowd had met on Kennington Common to march with O'Connor to take the petition to parliament but the large police presence meant the demonstrators were dispersed and O'Connor took the petition himself. This is what Source A is depicting.

Chapter 8
Page 41
SOURCE ANALYSIS

a The Corn Laws were introduced to help keep wheat prices high in Britain after the French war. The wealthy landowners who made up the government did not want any competition that would lower the price of wheat and reduce the profits they made.

b You should make your own revision cards.

c Peel's attitude to the Corn Laws was that they should be stopped as they prevented free trade. He also did not think that the government should control imports – he thought people should be able to buy wheat from any country, not just Britain.

d Being the leader of the Conservative Party caused Peel problems when he tried to repeal the Corn Laws as the Conservative Party was made up of rich landowners who wanted the price of wheat to stay high, as they made more money. If Peel acted too quickly he could run the risk of his party turning against him.

e Source A is useful to a historian studying the campaign to repeal the Corn Laws as it shows the role of key individuals such as Richard Cobden and Robert Peel. Cobden was an MP and a founder of the Anti-Corn Law League. The League was very organised and used the penny post to contact every eligible voter in Britain. Peel, the prime minister, supported the League, however he was the leader of the Tory Party who were mostly landowners who benefited from the Corn Laws. Therefore Peel could not be as pro-active as Cobden and this is what the cartoon is showing. The pair are walking in the direction of 'free trade' as can be seen on the sign in the background. Both the Anti-Corn Law League and Peel were supporters of free trade and this was a major motivation for the repeal in 1846.

Page 43
SIMILARITY

a People joined the Abolition Movement out of a moral duty: they were campaigning for reform for the 'white slaves' in British factories, so they should want to free the slaves being used by the British in the West Indies and America. Another reason was religious belief, as many felt treating people this way was not humane and therefore not Christian.

b Your mind-map could include: pamphlets, speeches, poems, writing.

c Answers might include the following similarities:

Supporters: both had support from the middle class

Methods used: speeches, pamphlets

Role of government: both movements had support in parliament: Wilberforce for the Abolition Movement and Peel for the Anti-Corn Law League.

Both were influenced by other events: famine and the conditions in British factories

Outcomes: both were a success and achieved their aims.

Page 45
FACTORS

a You might include the following:

communication: reports, had their own newspapers, penny post

religion: used religion to show that people were equal

politics: campaigned to have acts repealed, petitions, speeches in parliament

b Your plan should consider the following:

Communication: Anti-Corn Law League (penny post, railways), Chartists (newspapers), Abolition Movement (pamphlets)

Politics: Abolition Movement (speeches in parliament), Social (Josephine Butler, Chadwick), Anti-Corn Law League (support of Peel)

Religion: Abolition Movement (religious messages to remind people that everyone is equal)

Overall judgement about the most important factor

c **Communication:** Communication was the most important factor for bringing about reform in the nineteenth century as it allowed more people to be aware of campaigns and to join them. The Anti-Corn Law League's campaign used the penny post to contact all eligible voters. The Chartists created their own newspapers to spread their aims and encourage people to take action. Similarly, the abolition movement sent out pamphlets to the public with drawings of the conditions on slave ships to persuade people that slavery was wrong.

Politics: Politics was an important factor too. William Wilberforce used his platform as an MP to give speeches about the abolition of the slave trade resulting in the 1833 Abolition Act. Similarly, the Anti-Corn Law League leaders were MPs and had the support and influence of Robert Peel, ultimately leading to the repeal of the Corn Laws in 1846.

Religion: Religion had only a small role to play. Although many of the reformers were motivated by their faith the only reformers who used religion to influence support and reform were the abolitionists. Their badges, pamphlets and speeches reminded people

that everyone was equal under God, to persuade people to support the movement.

Conclusion: It's up to you which factor you decide was the most important, but make sure that you explain a clear reason for your opinion. For example, you could argue that communication was the most important because by reaching lots of people with the penny post and using the railway the Anti-Corn Law League gained so much more support. The same is true of the Chartists' use of newspapers and the abolitionists' use of pamphlets. Although it is important that some reformers could influence parliament directly, without the support and pressure of the public most reform would not have taken place.

Chapter 9
Page 47
SOURCE ANALYSIS

a Trade unionism is when workers form a body or bodies that they can join to help protect or improve their pay and conditions.

b You could have cards with the following information on them:

GNCTU – strikes, demonstrations

Tolpuddle Martyrs – oaths, strikes

New Model Unions – negotiating with employers

New Unionism – strikes, demonstrations

Match Girls – strikes, petitions, newspaper articles

Dockers – strikes, pickets, marches and demonstrations

c Your answer might include the following:

- The source is useful because it shows workers marching and demonstrating. These were tactics used by New Unionism, along with the GNCTU at their march at Copenhagen Fields.
- The source shows the marchers representing their unions and carrying union banners. New unions helped to organise the workers, such as the match girls who went on strike with the help of the journalist, Annie Besant.

Chapter 10
Page 49
SOURCE ANALYSIS

a • The government used force – you can see this as the woman is being held down.
- They put women in prison – the woman is clearly in a jail cell.
- They force-fed women – the woman has a tube going down her nose.

b The artist wants us to feel shocked and sorry for the suffragette as she is being held around the neck and being force-fed. The purpose of the poster is to make us support the suffragettes – we are reminded of their aims by the message on the jail wall.

c Source A is useful to a historian a studying the government responses to the suffragettes as it shows a woman in jail being force-fed. The suffragettes were frequently arrested as their tactics became more militant. It was at this time that they would target buildings and MPs as a way to be noticed and gain the vote. The source shows that the government were willing to use force as can be seen from the three people holding the suffragette down. Suffragettes were force-fed in prison until the Cat and Mouse Act was introduced in 1913.

Page 51

SIGNIFICANCE

a Women did not have the vote. They were thought to belong in the home and were still seen as too temperamental and emotional to handle the world of politics.

b You could select five of the following dates/events:

- **First World War:** The suffragettes stopped campaigning for the vote and joined the war effort. It was during the war that the first Representation of the People Act, 1918 gave some women over the age of 30 the vote.
- **1928:** Women gained the vote on equal terms with men.
- **1960s:** The Women's Movement: Campaigned for greater equality – to give women the same rights as men.
- **1969 Divorce Reform Act:** this gave women the right to divorce their husbands which meant they had more control of their lives.
- **1970 Equal Pay Act:** Women could now expect to be paid the same as men for the same work.
- **1975 Sex Discrimination Act:** women could no longer be treated differently in the workplace because of their gender.

c This is your opinion, but remember that the event having the biggest impact could be a turning point – a moment that brings about a major change.

d The suffragette movement was significant because it changed social attitudes towards women. Many people had argued that politics was a man's world and not for women as they were too temperamental. However, by stopping their campaign to help with the war effort during the First World War they showed that they were level-headed and capable of dealing with difficult situations as they worked as nurses, in factories and on the land.

Another way the movement is significant is the impact it had on politics. The suffragettes campaigned from the creation of the WSPU in 1903 by using militant tactics to get the attention of the government. It was this, along with their war work, that led to a change in the law, firstly in 1918 and then finally with the Representation of the People Act, 1928, which saw women gain the vote on equal terms with men.

The new ideas of equality can be seen during the Women's Movement in the 1970s when women fought for equality in all areas of life.

Chapter 11
Page 53

FACTORS

a Creating their own newspaper, strikes, demonstrations, marches

b Your flashcards should have key government responses on one side and then the impacts linked to them on the other. For example, you could write '1927 Trades Disputes and Trade Unions Act' on the front of one card with the reverse stating 'This act stopped trade unions being able to join together to strike or pay funds to a political party. This meant that the unions could lose political support.'

c Your answer should choose from the following:

- **Communication:** newspapers, petitions, speeches
- **Economy:** subsidies, TUC ran out of money, price of coal
- **Politics:** changes in the law and governments

Chapter 12
Page 55

SOURCE ANALYSIS

a The cartoon shows a black family, looking fed up, outside a house with a sign that says 'No Entry'. They have all their luggage with them showing they have not found anywhere to settle.

b The message is that black immigrants were finding it hard to find accommodation and were not able to settle in Britain. The caption also lets us know that the Commonwealth was not seen as a good thing by everyone at this point.

c By 1961 a lot of people from the Caribbean and Asia had arrived in Britain. Anti-immigrant feeling had increased and clashes had started between white and non-white communities. There were issues around housing and employment for the immigrants, and segregation.

d Anti-immigrant feeling had become such a problem that the new Commonwealth Immigrant Acts were being passed through parliament (first act passed in 1962). They were designed to limit the amount of immigration from Commonwealth countries to the UK. The series of reforms that followed showed that the British government wanted to change immigration and many people saw these changes as being against black people.

e You can use your answers to parts **a** to **d** to answer this question. You may want to add that the source is useful because the cartoonist worked for the *Evening Standard*, a London newspaper. This shows that government responses to immigration were important and were having an impact on society.

Page 57

SIMILARITY

a The bubbles of your mind-map should include the following details:

Political: The rise of extreme political groups like the National Front and the politics of Enoch Powell.

Social: Poor relations with police. There was a feeling that young black men were victims of racial profiling because of 'sus law'.

Economic: The recession had a big impact on poor black communities, with unemployment, poor housing and increased crime.

b In the short term, the Brixton Riots resulted in the Scarman Report, which reviewed the actions of the police and created the Police Complaints Authority. It also ended 'sus law'. In the long term it put the Metropolitan Police under more pressure after the murder of Stephen Lawrence.

c The people who rioted in Brixton are similar to the suffragettes when considering the methods they used. Both used violence to protest the way they were being treated by the government and by the police. In Brixton they set fire to cars and buildings and fought with the police. This is similar to the suffragettes, who had an arson campaign and attacked buildings and the police.

Another similarity is that both the people who rioted in Brixton and the suffragettes changed government policy. In the case of Brixton there was the removal of 'sus law' which was to end racial profiling. Because of the suffragettes, the Representation of the People Act 1918 saw women over the age of 30 who owned property being allowed to vote. Furthermore, the groups are similar as the government reactions alone were not enough to gain equality. It would take women until 1928 to gain the vote on equal terms with men, and after the death of Stephen Lawrence in 1993 the Metropolitan Police Service was found to suffer from institutional racism.

A

aristocratic: being part of the ruling class or the nobility

autocrat: ruler who holds all the power

B

ballot: slip of paper used to register a vote, completed in secret

baron: man who had been given high rank by the king; the title came with land

burgess: person who owned land or a house in a burgh; like peasants they were bound to their Lord

C

cavalry: soldiers on horseback

colony: country or area under the full or partial control of another country and occupied by settlers from that country

Congress: national legislative body in the USA that makes laws

constitution: written document stating how a country or state is to be governed

D

democracy: system of government which gives everyone a say by allowing them to vote for people to represent them in parliament

divine right: idea that a person (such as a king) has been appointed by God, and has the right to make any decision and not be questioned, as they are God's representative on earth

E

empire: collection of tribes, regions, territories, states or countries that are ruled over and controlled by one leader or 'mother country'; the areas controlled are usually called colonies (although sometimes dominions or dependencies; the mother country makes many of the key decisions to do with the places it rules over.

F

feudal system: Medieval system of land holding and distribution in which the use of the land is paid for by performing services and work for the owner

freeman: peasant in the feudal system who rented land from a landowner for an agreed fee; different from unfree peasants who had to provide services to the landowner in exchange for the land that they used

free trade: trade that is not restricted by governments

G

groat: silver coin worth four English pennies

I

infantry: soldiers who fight on foot

J

Justice of the Peace: local official appointed by the king, responsible for law and order

L

laissez-faire: French words meaning 'leave alone'; in the nineteenth century many people felt that this was what the government should do: not interfere, not force people to change, and allow things to take their own course

Laudian: something done by William Laud

M

martyr: person who dies for their cause and becomes a symbol for a movement or a cause

merchant: person who buys and sells goods

Model Parliament: first parliament to resemble ours today; it had representatives from the Church and the aristocracy as well as those from the counties and boroughs (commoners)

N

nationalise: when the government takes control of owns an industry or a service

O

orator: person who is considered an expert public speaker

P

pardon: act of forgiving a crime

parliament: group of people responsible for making laws

penal colony: place of imprisonment and punishment at a remote location

petition: request to do or change something, normally presented to government; people sign one to show how much support the request has

philanthropist: person who donates their time and money to charitable causes

picket: to stand outside or near a workplace and try to persuade other workers not to enter the workplace

pious: deeply religious, observing religion completely

providence: God's intervention in the world; people who believe that something is divine providence believe that God wants something to happen

purge: physical removal of something or someone; normally carried out violently or abruptly

Puritan: hard-line Protestant Christian who believes in simple church services and lifestyles; Puritans protested against the practices of the Catholic Church

R

racial profiling: when police target an individual for a crime, based purely on their race

recession: period when the economy of a country or the world is poor; this can mean an increase in unemployment

Reformation: the 'break with Rome' by Henry VIII in 1534, when he made England's official religion Protestantism rather than Catholicism

repeal: remove or reverse (a law)

republic: country with a system of government where an elected President has supreme power, rather than a monarch

S

scutage: tax collected during wartime; normally paid by a knight instead of completing military service

siege: military blockade common in Medieval battles; usually done to starve out an opponent

Star Chamber: court where people who had gone against the king were tried; run by supporters of the king

T

temperance: moderate intake of, or complete abstinence from, alcohol

Tory: the Tory Party of the nineteenth century believed in a strong Britain and free trade

W

Whig: member of a political party that believed in the power of parliament; the Whig party was important in reforming parliament

Notes